T

Teaching English in South Korea

A Guide and Critique of Teaching English in South Korea

Know before you go!

Dwight H. Gauer

Teaching English in South Korea
Copyright © 2013 by Dwight H. Gauer

Photo Credits: Interior photos by Dwight H. Gauer unless otherwise noted.
Interior comics by Luke Martin

ISBN – 978-1-49-040159-1
   9 781490-401591

Printed in U.S.A

Foreword by David Park

Acknowledgements

To all of my wonderful students, past and present, this book would not have been possible without you!

Table of Contents

Foreword

By David Park

The thought that first came to me as I began to read Teaching English in South Korea was that there was no way I would put my name on such a polemical book. I do, after all, have my reputation to consider. However, after coming to terms with that thought, I began to see the forest through the trees. Although the book is sure to arouse ire among some because of its take-no-prisoners writing style, it does at least attempt to take an honest look at what happens and what to expect in various teaching environments in South Korea.

The author related to me the many expats living in South Korea who, after reading the book, refused to write a foreword. To those expats I say, "Grow some balls." And, although I do not agree with everything the author has written in this tell-all book, I certainly understand his position given that he has lived in Korea for 17 years, was married to a Korean national, and has 2 sons from that marriage.

As a retired teacher who spent many, many years teaching in South Korea, I heartily recommend this book to anyone who is considering teaching in South Korea. Even if readers find that South Korea is not for them, the book still manages to convey very important information regarding teaching overseas; including methodologies, texts, teaching children, and so much more.

David Park
CEO - Jobs-Korea.org

Preface

It is no secret that English in S. Korea has been on a tear of late. Seems everywhere one looks in Korea, one sees or hears English. It's on T-shirts, print and screen advertising, pop songs, TV programs, books, cars and trucks, restaurants, bars. In addition, the Korean government, nationally and locally, enacts English language programs that hire native speakers to teach in many venues. It's taught at universities, language institutes, city halls, elementary, secondary and high schools; trade schools, corporations, centers for the elderly, and many more. It's audience? Nearly everyone from all ages to all professions.

To put things into perspective, Korea spends more per capita on English language education than any other country in the world. Even so, Korea still trails other nations in English fluency.

The first thing you should know about English in Korea is that it is not learned for enjoyment, but rather a tool for gaining entrance to one of the top 10 universities. Also, Korean parents, particularly the Tiger Mother, will willingly spend thousands of dollars on private English education each year. This madness is not without warrant. Korea places much - far too much - importance on English language study as you will soon come to find. This importance does not end at high school graduation. It is recognized by university students and professionals alike. Obviously, this contributes to the economic burden of Korean families; a burden, to this author, really shouldn't exist in the first place.

It is currently believed, correctly, by many of the officialdom and others that inadequate English-language education creates various problems, including excessive money wasted on private institutes, so-called ``goose fathers" sending their wives and children to English-speaking countries, and unqualified foreign tutors and teachers.

I can't recall the reference, but one ministry of education official has said that because of the flawed educational system, students are forced to enroll in private education institutes or overseas study. Naturally, this results in an imbalance in English ability between those who attend these institutes and those who do not as you will discover shortly.

Indeed, there seems to be no end in sight to this English language boom. Demand continues to be robust and supply constraints continue to be of concern. Naturally, the increased need for English fluency is due to globalization; Korea is no different than any country that wishes to have an English fluent workforce, which is yet another sizable reason for this continued demand growth for English language teachers.

Purpose of this Book

Because we are still in the middle of this English language boom, writing this book could not be timelier. My goal is to inform and allow you, oh dear reader, to make an informed decision as to whether or not you think you might like to come to Korea and have a go at it. Before you consider that, you must be aware that one of the most often quoted pieces of advice from current and former English teachers in Korea: *be prepared, come with an open mind, and do your homework.* Whether you are an experienced or inexperienced teacher, or simply looking for a career path, I am confident that this book will provide you with insightful information and convincing reasons as to why you may want to participate in the English language boom or, conversely, why you may not want to participate. Last, this book will also provide you with many ways in which to participate in the English language boom.

Interestingly, when I was first approached about writing this book, I struggled with the direction and focus. I knew that I wanted to write about this English language fervor that I have so adamantly proclaimed over the last ten to 15 years, but I was wondering who my target audience would be, and what I wanted them to take away from the book. I quickly realized that many potential language teachers lack a basic understanding about teaching English in Korea. That is, they might know about teaching English in a general sense, but they don't really know how Korean society functions and where and how to participate. If they did, they would have participated many years ago. I also found out that this lack of understanding is often compounded by the fact that many people have misconceptions about teaching English in Korea. Because of misconceptions, many teachers have shied away from

Korea, despite some prolific improvements in this market. For this reason, it was important for me to write a book that provides the foundation for how English language works and is taught in Korea, why it is so integral to many Korean's daily lives, and how English language teaching in Korea can not only provide teachers with an opportunity to join me, but also give them some sense of balance when coming to Korea.

Inevitably, in a short book of such a sweeping nature, there are many hostages to critics. Nevertheless, this is a book that I feel needs to be written and discussed.

How This Book Is Organized

As a result, it was quite clear that I had to focus on establishing the case for teaching English in Korea from the ground up. While some of the content will be basic for experienced teachers already in Korea, it is necessary and fundamental for the new teacher. Indeed, teachers who simply want to learn more about the teaching market in an easy-to-understand way will find this book even more rewarding.

Besides wanting to write a book that describes teaching English in Korea clearly, I also wanted to provide a backdrop for the different ways of participating in the many venues available to teachers. I realize that many teachers have different career goals and may want to tap into this long-term language boom because it offers teachers career advancement that they may not have in other markets.

In Part Two, "Participating in the Teaching Market," I look at the various documents that readers will need to study. Specifically, I delve into questions readers may have regarding teaching contracts, visa documents, sample lesson plans at the public school level, and my real-life experiences teaching children, which is perhaps the most important unit in this book. I also wanted to outline what readers will need to participate in Korea. I say outline because there is a wealth of information on the internet regarding the subject. Just so, my outline is based on my, and that of others, experience who have participated in Korean culture for over ten years, so it has a unique twist.

Taking the time to learn about the venues and the advantages/disadvantages that they offer today can better help you position yourself to profit from the moves of programs that will no doubt occur in the future. And by the time you finish reading this book, I hope you will have a firm understanding of why you would, or would not, like to join me in Korea.

Let me add that the real issue, one that has challenged me since the beginning of this book, was to weed the non-essentials. There exists an information overload about teaching English in Korea, and if you begin to research teaching in Korea, which I don't recommend, (just email, Skype or ask on seonsang.com) you're going to go into cognitive overload mode in a heartbeat. Each and every one of us living and working in Korea has an opinion on nearly every conceivable aspect of this country and its people. Therefore, you had better value my opinion most because I've lived and worked here for a very long time. I was married to a Korean woman for 17 years and have 2 sons from that marriage. My sons are in middle and elementary school, so I have unique knowledge and insight into the structure of those schools. Finally, you must learn to disregard the opinions of others who have lived here for only a few years as they have very little insight into the culture, teaching or otherwise, of Korea. Many of them have axes to grind, so it can be extremely difficult to make impartial observations concerning their remarks about teaching in Korea.

Last, this book is *not* value judgment free. I do have strong opinions about teaching English in Korea and I cannot simply disseminate teaching from culture. I make no apologies about my value judgments, nor do I wish to.

Try to remember that, also.

Abbreviations and Acronyms

NSET	Native Speaker English Teacher
KET	Korean English Teacher
MOE	Ministry of Education
POE	Provincial Office of Education
CSAT	The Korean Scholastic Aptitude Test
OPIc	Oral Proficiency Interview by Computer
EFL	English as a Foreign Language
ESL	English as a Second Language
IMF	International Monetary Fund
TOEIC	Test of English Language for International Communication
TOEFL	Test of English as a Foreign Language

Teaching English in South Korea

Part One

UNDERSTANDING THE DEMAND FOR THE ENGLISH LANGUAGE

Chapter 1

The English Language Boom

Why It's Here and Why It's Going to Last

As stated in the introduction, there exists in Korea an English fervor close to fanaticism that has been around for as long as I can remember. The former president of Korea, Lee Myung-bak, was one of those fanatics, much to the dismay of many Korean English teachers (KETs). He had been promoting English in the schools like none other. Lee wanted Korea to be more English-friendly and believed that having every high school graduate conversational in English was the way to get there.

A quick look what Lee wanted:

• He proposed not only to have all English classes taught in English, but to have core subjects, such as science and math, taught in English as well. This policy has been abandoned - not enough fluent Korean teachers and simply too much teacher protest.

• Planned to expand English class hours at elementary schools. As of this writing, 3rd and 4th graders have English class for one hour per week, and 5th graders, 2 hours. The government planned to increase the class by one or two hours per week, which has been implemented.

You may well be thinking, what has that to do with you? Well, it's quite obvious that an increase in English instruction equals an increase in teachers. To that end, have a look at the next bullet.

• A new employment plan of 23,000 English teachers for English-only classes. The majority of these teachers should be Koreans. This plan was scrapped, as have many other employment plans. No need to worry, however, there will always be hundreds, if not thousands of new NSET hires every year long into the future.

Prior to assuming office, the former president was very concerned regarding income and English proficiency levels, i.e., parents who are well-off spending enormous amounts of money every month for their children's' private education. Just so, not every parent can afford to do this, thus an income disparity exists between those who have and those who don't. This concern is not groundless when one considers that almost all mid-to-high income jobs require high proficiency in English (or, at least a test-score to that effect).

It's too early to tell what the policies of the current president, Park Geun-hye, regarding English will be. Just so, it's a safe bet that she, too, will express similar fervor towards English that her predecessor did. Time will tell.

It's a Bull Market

I am, obviously, using the stock market as an analogy to teaching English in Korea. Quite simply we are in a roaring bull market in teaching. This is not a bubble. This bull market has existed for 20 years and shows no signs of letting up. So long as Korea, similar to many other developed/developing countries, undergoes globalization, language teaching will grow exponentially over the years to come. The World Bank calls it the *"massification"* of English; if not Korea, then a host of other nations. China, for example, is fast becoming one of the best places to find employment as an English teacher. Once I get wind that this factor has changed, I might consider changing my position. For now, though, demand factors are very much in place and are not waning.

Consequently, the continued supply and demand imbalance facing the teaching markets today will not only propel this bull market further but will also translate to potentially the greatest teaching opportunity our generation will ever know.

Remember that, also.

Chapter 2

The Korean Educational System

Education either functions as an instrument which is used to facilitate integration of the younger generation into the logic of the present system and bring about conformity or it becomes the practice of freedom, the means by which men and women deal critically and creatively with reality and discover how to participate in the transformation of their world.

---Paulo Friere

B efore you begin your journey through this treatise, an introduction to the educational culture in Korea is absolutely necessary. Once you begin to understand the educational culture, you'll be better positioned to participate in it, which will lead to less stress, cultural misunderstandings, and, perhaps, allow you to become a better and more effective teacher. Allow me to preface this by stating that there are more than a few topics in this book that could easily become books in and of themselves. This topic is one of them. That said, I'll try not to waste your time, and get to the heart of the matter using as little print as possible.

That Koreans place a great amount of importance on education is a monumental understatement. However, as

Mr. Friere so succinctly points out in the above quote, there are two kinds of education. Korean education is of the first type: students learn to conform; which may be the result of centuries of Confucian influence. Koreans have a borrowed proverb: the nail that stands up gets hammered down. Freedom of expression and individualism are not Korean mores; conformity and what's good for the collective are. There are exceptions to this, but they are micro-exceptions; expressions of individuality beyond the collective good that are, at their worst, highly toxic.

Education, during the **Joseon Dynasty** (Chosŏn) - 1392 – 1897, had as its primary goal the preparation of students of the ruling class or nobles for civil service. The civil service examinations, known as gwageo, were rigorous examinations in which students put their noses to the grindstone because to pass these exams meant an envious position and high status; two of the most prevalent goals of learning at that time. Thus, it can be said that Koreans have placed high import on education for attaining status and power for centuries. Going forward, one sees that these notions of education are still very much alive and well.

Indeed, Korea, to this author, is an exam nightmare. I sometimes think one needs to pass an exam simply to cross the street.

You've already read some facts and figures regarding learning English in Korea, but they barely touch the surface of the matter. To that end, I'll begin by outlining the system.

Korea uses the following school system: 6-3-3-4. Six years of elementary, three years of middle school, three years of high school, and four years of university education. The higher education institutions consist of graduate schools, four-year universities, and two or three-year junior colleges.

6

No mention is made of preschool, but it is very much alive and well. Back in the 1970s and 1980s there were really only a handful of preschools scattered across the nation; preschool was just beginning to catch on. These days, you'll find them everywhere. The last figure I read was from 2010; there were roughly 9,000 preschools. Most, if not all, tuition for preschools is subsidized by the Korean government for low-income families because preschools are not wholly government administered. This is a positive move because it allows every child access to preschool regardless of economic status. Kindergarten education is carried out in national, public, and private kindergartens for preschool children ages three to five

Elementary school (*chodeung-hakgyo*) attendance is an astounding 100 percent. I've seen figures quoted by the Korean Ministry of Education stating that the number of students per teachers in the elementary schools is currently 28.1, and the average number of students per class was 34.9 (2002). Beginning in 1996, English has been taught as a part of the regular curriculum.

Unlike American schools, students aren't given letter grades. Rather, scores are based on a percentage system. For example, you can score a maximum 100 percent in an English class. Let's have a look at what I'm talking about here:

Mid-Terms	30%
Finals	30%
Speaking	10%
Writing	10%
Listening	10% (based on a government exam)

However, the most fundamental difference between American and Korean schools is that you *don't* need to pass your classes to matriculate to the next grade level (so much for the boastful 98 percent high school graduation rate.) Thus, students can be absolute *blockheads* but won't be held back a grade because of poor scores. This is also true of middle and high school students. After six years of elementary education, students aged twelve to fourteen move on to three years - seventh to ninth grade - of middle school.

Upon completion of middle school, students begin the unmitigated hell know as high school. It's said that there are two types of high schools in Korea, general and vocational. But, I believe I could add a third school; a special type for students with issues or who simply find the general high schools troubling. The vo-ed schools are agriculture, technical, commercial, fishing and oceanography. Students who wish to enter the vo-ed schools do so by examinations given by each school. They have a choice of which vocation they would like to pursue, such as commerce, home economics, engineering, agriculture, and maritime studies. Ordinarily, 40 – 60 percent of curriculum is devoted to general studies and the rest general courses.

Not all general high schools are the same. There are also specialized schools offering such specializations as the arts, science, foreign languages, and physical education. The reason for these schools is obvious; if students have talent in any of these fields, they can focus on them.

The former administration also began what are known as *"garden schools"* and schools in rural communities that board students, so they will stay in their communities and not migrate to the cities. Furthermore, there are also high schools that let students find work right out of high school and enroll into university later.

Finally, studies at general high schools, most common in Korea, focus on preparing students for the CSAT exam.

These are the schools in which students suffer from a variety of educational maladies.

Just as in the USA, the Korean school year has two semesters. The first semester begins in the beginning of March and ends around the end of July. The second semester begins at the end of August, and runs to the beginning of January.

As an aside, I find the Ministry of Education's credos for high school education somewhat humorous: "High school education is mainly aimed at first, raising the ability to pioneer one's own career path that fits individual aptitude and talent based upon the outcome of education and second, developing the capacity required for becoming a global citizen." Not only that, but these,

1) To form a balanced character supported by a sound mind and body and to have a mature sense of self

2) To acquire the ability to think and attitudes that are logical, critical, and creative to be prepared for the world of learning and living

3) To be trained in the knowledge and skills of various fields and to develop the ability to pioneer one's career path in a way that fits individual aptitudes and talents.

4) To seek the development of Korea's tradition and culture in the context of the world

5) To work for development of the national community and to have the awareness and attitude of a global citizen.

I find these tenants enormously entertaining because Korean general high schools are glorified cram schools whose primary goal is to prepare students for the CSAT – college entrance exam - nothing more, nothing less.

Finally, the universities and colleges of which there are an assortment: general four-year schools, teacher's universities, two-year vocational colleges, an air and correspondence university, open universities, and many others that offer two or four-year programs such as nursing schools, and theological schools. Back in 2002, there were 358 institutions of higher learning! That, readers, is incredible for such a small country. Before Korea's disastrous economic crash in 1997, universities were springing up everywhere, and they had no problem filling desks with students. After the crash, in which IMF bailed out Korea, things began to change as did the universities themselves. Enrollment dropped, forcing schools to unite or drastically change their fields of study. Worst of all, many began to accept any warm body, regardless of CSAT scores, to avoid closure.

Placement and acceptance at most universities for students is determined by high school records and the CSAT. However, there are a few schools that administer an entrance essay test on top of those. I've detailed institutes of higher learning within the book, so no more will be said on the subject.

Dancing with the Tiger

Child abuse is one of the most widespread types of violence tolerated. It is so embedded in human culture that almost no country outlaws parents' violence against children. Only 16 countries (e.g. Austria, Finland, Norway, and Sweden) have established legislation that protects children from physical punishment.

--Global Initiative to End Corporal Punishment, 2006

While you read this book, you're going to see a lot of "Tiger Mother, Tiger Teacher." Korea is home to both. Korean teachers, for the most part, are simply an extension of what occurs in the home: Tiger Teachers emulate Tiger Mothers. This is based on the traditional school system in

Korea which was primarily influenced by China. Over time, Koreans learned Confucianism at school and came to accept the "Tiger" concept of education as the norm. After the Korean War, the school system underwent dramatic changes primarily influenced while under Western (mostly the USA) occupation. So, these days we seem to have a blend of East/West. Nevertheless, the Tiger system is alive and well; make no mistake.

It really is beyond the scope of this book to debate the east/west dichotomy, but to really grasp what this system demands of its children, we need to devote at least a minuscule amount of time to the subject so as to allow you maximum insight into the minds of Korean students, teachers, and mothers.

If you're not already familiar with the term, a Tiger Mother is one who micro-manages her children, treats failure as a reflection of personal failure, is obsessed with grades to the point of absurdity, does not accept compromise with her spouse regarding her patterns of conduct, is unable to think for herself, and flies into a rage when her children do not obey absolutely, or become hostile due to her policies. I often think how Tiger Mothers would fit hand in glove as willing participants in Nazi Germany. Strong opinion, yes, but I feel you will come to agree as you read on.

There have been books written on the subject, both in defense and offense of the Tiger Mother. My take on this phenomenon is that it is culturally dependent; Tigers in Korea, Japan, and China, for example really miss the big picture; once their children enter university, freedom, self-rebellion, and the pursuit of lost childhood primary, which leads to sub-average students, particularity in Korea. This has been my experience at more than one Korean university. Thus, you'll understand why I call many Korean universities *adult daycare centers*. One exception to this are students who return from their mandatory military service; these students are a delight to teach.

Moreover, at least for this Tiger Mother's ex-spouse (Panda dad), is the fact that children learn nothing about *life beyond the book*. I was fortunate to have a wonderfully rich childhood. My dad took us boys hunting, fishing, hiking, taught us how to build furniture, boats, houses; taught us to drive when we were 9 years old, play baseball, football, basketball; bought us bikes, motorcycles ,cars and how to repair them, and, most important, taught us about women. It's little wonder, then, that I have an overabundance of confidence and self-reliance. Conversely, 14 hours of studying math, science and piano do none of the above. I would hazard that having a Tiger Mother in Korean society is a death knell to becoming independent, self-reliant, and knowledgeable beyond what is taught in books. And, as a result, Korean males know little about the flip side of potential beyond books. Most couldn't build a simple piece of furniture, bait a hook, plant a garden, or indulge in physical labor. If physical labor must be done, it is done begrudgingly. In short, they are not men that I would be proud of.

Tiger Mothers also exhibit control issues. In an attempt to control their own lives, they exert control over others, which often leads to disastrous results. They often go to great lengths to achieve whatever control over those around them through the exercise of control and manipulation. Gone are skills many hold in high regard: negotiation and endurance of rejection or failure.

Further damning evidence of what Korea's emphasis on knowledge rather than social skills can be found in a report by the Korean Educational Development Institute and the National Youth Policy Institute. The report was based on a survey of roughly 146,000 eighth grade students conducted in 2009 by the International Association for the Evaluation of Educational Achievement. Korean students scored an average of 0.31 out of 1.0 for social interaction skills. This average placed Korea at 35th out of 36 nations that took part in the survey. What does this mean? Simply that Korean student's social skills are nearly the worst in the world. So when it comes to getting along with others, Korean teens fail miserably. Arguably, this is due to the fact that Korean youth learn so little about the world and so much about subjects other than human relations.

Not only that, but competition among students intense, also. With that in mind, it is little wonder that they are so terrible at social interaction. Thank you again, Tiger mom/ Tiger teacher.

Yes, the children of Tigers are sometimes successful, if they don't commit suicide first. As of May, 2012 at least 11 teens have committed suicide due to stress over grades, according to the Seoul Metropolitan Office of Education. As mentioned previously, success in Korea means admittance to one of the top 10 universities, scoring a prestigious position within the government, and making boat-loads of money. Never mind that they must unhappily slog away for the rest of their lives on a job they scorn. Ask a Korean if he likes his job, and he'll look at you like you should be instituted.

Evidence of this can be found in a research done by TNS, a market-research firm. They found that Koreans are decidedly more dissatisfied with their jobs than folks from other nations. The research found that only half had anything positive to say about the companies they work for, compared to three-quarters of the research's results for other countries. And, quite frankly, I would rather cut my wrists than become a wage slave in Korea. Due to its hierarchical structure, Korean blue and white collar alike give a big middle finger to those in control; and that, friends, is why Soju (Korean alcohol) exists.

Recall the Western saying, *"If you love what you do, you will never work a day in your life."* And, yes, I'm aware that this expression can be much debated – less money, over-saturation. Despite those arguments, such a saying is beyond the Korean reality, as is the fact that the path to fulfillment, whether career or life in general, is fraught with peril and requires endless trial and error.

As for the daughters of Tiger Mothers, I have very little to admire. Many Korean girls become women that are highly conformist (future Tigers?) and boring at best. Very few take the time to self-actualize and find outside interests, which would make them much more interesting people. Their path is well-trampled: get married, have children, die...hell, I forgot watch TV, eat, and sleep. But perhaps that is the whole point to their happiness: be comfortable and find solace in predictably.

That Western parents allow their children too much freedom cannot be denied. Obviously, what is needed is a blend of both camps. I think Tiger countries like Korea do offer Western parents insight and options into their own educational philosophies. I believe that Western parents do want to get tougher on education and become a hell of a lot more involved; they just don't know how to go about it because they're far too interested in making friends with their children. Children do want to be good at most things, whether it be baseball, math, or music. From my experience, they really do want someone to teach them how to be better, how to improve.

For sake of clarity, one of the goals of education is that it is supposed to prepare us for is individual growth, maturity and plenitude to be the unique persons we are, not to live another's life or dreams. This goal has no meaning and is far too idealistic for the win/lose, two alternative Tiger Mother.

While doing research for divorce in Korea, I came across a story in one of the English language newspapers in Korea regarding a Korean husband who divorced his Tiger wife because she would beat their son whenever he scored poorly on exams. For a Korean male to divorce his wife because she is a Tiger is unheard of. My hat is off to this brave soul!

Obama your mama and birds in the belfry

You may or may not have heard the words, somewhat inexplicably, of praise for the Korea educational system when President Obama visited Korea in 2011. *"Our children spend over a month less in school than children in South Korea every year. That's no way to prepare them for a 21st century economy."* I won't argue his statement, but in Korea, folks were simply puzzled. Korean parents couldn't be less skeptical of the public school system. This skepticism has given wings to *goose fathers* wherein the father stays in Korea and works to support his wife and children overseas. If he has the finances, he can do a migratory visit to his overseas family annually and become an *eagle father*; if not, he is called a *penguin father* and must endure privations that are extremely unfortunate: poor nutrition, abject loneliness, clinical depression. The *"bird"* phenomenon really took off in the late 1990s, due to dissatisfaction with the school system's hyper-competitiveness and the desire to learn English well. Currently, there are about 100,000 Koreans studying abroad. But that is just the beginning; the system also gave way to private tutoring, cram schools, sub-average teachers and students, and never-ending debate of public education reform.

In a 2008 survey by South Korea's National Statistical Office, 48.3 percent of South Korean parents said they wanted to send their children abroad to *"develop global perspectives,"* avoid the rigid domestic school system, or learn English. More than 12 percent wanted it for their children as early as elementary school

Not only that, students *also* distrust the public school system. Many high school students have stated that if they have a question, they don't ask their public school teachers, they ask their cram school teachers. Worst of all, public school dissatisfaction has given rise to corporate thievery such as megastudy.com, which is simply a harbinger of things to come regarding online cram schools.

Evidence of parental dissatisfaction can be seen in the Global Competitiveness Report for 2010—2011, in which the World Economic Forum surveyed 39 economies worldwide. One of the questions, as measured by domestic opinion polling, was *quality of primary education*. Korea ranked 31st. Korea's overall rank for a dozen other educational related criteria was 22nd. This is damning evidence for parental distrust of the public educational system in Korea, and what drives parents into extreme education.

But let's return to Obama. He also stated in his State of the Union Address last year that South Korean teachers are known as *"nation builders."* I don't know where in hell he got his information, but I cannot find any reference to it for the life of me, nor can my Korean friends. I suspect, as per usual, that it was political in nature. At that time, Obama and company were attempting to push through the Korea-USA FTA. Another reason, far more critical, was the cabinet's agenda of nuclear non-proliferation. Anyway you analyze it, it's just plain stupid.

Byong Man-Ahn, the former minister of education, science, and technology in South Korea had this to say at meeting of the Association for Education Finance and Policy in Seattle. "*Although the pain of memorizing is unavoidable for young students to acquire new knowledge, they should also be motivated by the pleasure of creative expression*," Mr. Ahn told the audience. "*However, we force the students to memorize so much that they experience pain rather than pleasure [of] acquiring knowledge through the learning process.*"

And this from Education Minister Lee Ju-ho as told to Amanda Ripley of Time magazine, "*You Americans see a bright side of the Korean system, but Koreans are not happy with it.*"

Obama your mama...

Korean education officials are becoming more aware of the failures of their system. They are implementing many changes in hope that Korea will become less obsessed with the college entrance exam, rote memorization, and hagwons. Not too long ago, ministry officials began changing testing and university admissions policies in an attempt to lessen Korea's obsession for after-hours study. They seemed to be at least half-assed serious about rewarding forgotten qualities like creativity; although this author believes that it will do little good. Back in 2008, former president Lee said at his inauguration, "*One-size-fits-all, government-led uniform curriculum and an education system that is locked only onto the college-entrance examination are not acceptable,*" Yet, he and his cabinet did very little to improve the system. In fact, Lee pushed English study much harder than his predecessors.

However, in fairness to Lee, he was cognizant of a dysfunctional system by stating his regret for the endangered Korean tradition of "*dragons ascending from the sewers*" — intelligent children from poor families gaining envious positions in business and government, just as Lee did. And, "*These days, the rich get the help of cramming tutors and get good exam scores to enter colleges,*" he said. "*This discriminates against children who can't afford private education.*" Yet, for every new policy that attempts to tame the hagwon culture, the hagowns answer in kind by, for example, offering video on demand for all subjects.

Change will come slowly to Korea, but it will happen. How effective change will be is another thread.

Cramming by the Millions

Yet more disturbing figures: one hundred thousand cram schools give or take a few hundred, currently exist in Korea. These schools collectively earn about $15 billion annually. Yes, readers, you *can* become a millionaire teaching English! To wit, Andrew Kim, an instructor at Megastudy, a mega-hagwon/cram school based in Seoul, stated that he earned *$4 million* in 2010 from online and in-person lectures.

You will sometimes see (or experience) students sleeping in the back of the classroom in public school classrooms. This behavior is due to the student practice of *"studying ahead"* of the classes' curriculum; thus learning the material prior to teaching. This practice allows the student to excel in school and applies pressure on other families to *"keep up with the Lees."* That is, they want their children to excel in public school, also

This parental angst is what makes many hagwons and tutors very rich, much to my dismay. One tutor, who has nearly 50,000 students, online and offline, averages $6.8 million per year. She has dubbed herself "The Queen of English" This author would call her "The Queen of Parasites." People like this are parasites feeding on the anxiety of parents. Yet, the Korean government boneheads, in all their wisdom, do nothing to control this parasitical behavior.

Here in Korea, the anxiety that I refer to is actively stoked by hagwons; hagwons have one of the largest advertising budgets in Korea. You see advertisements on buses, billboards, fliers taped to your door, and newspapers catering to that same parental anxiety. And, naturally, the Tigers fall for these trendy ad copies without fail. If they didn't, their children wouldn't be privy to exam tips and tricks that perhaps other students have in their exam arsenal. Indeed, the Tiger's anxiety over her children's education means a steady stream of income for the private tutor and hagwon.

What is really sad is when hagwon students either fail to learn or learn very little due to tutors/teachers who lack content knowledge and pedagogical techniques. These tutors typically place all the blame on the student and none on themselves, and the Tiger Mother usually agrees with this analysis and continues to throw good money after bad.

Yet more damning evidence on cram schools can be found in a study done by Byun Soo-yong (2011). He used propensity score matching to find if there was indeed an improvement when the effect of tutoring was compared to academic achievement in mathematics for a nationally representative sample of lower secondary students. He discovered that hagwon cramming, when focused on test preparation, scored a very small difference in achievement gains. Conversely, private and internet tutoring made little difference. Other studies similar in nature to Byun's have been also shown poor results.

As a result, it's not unusual to find that students, particularly in high school, often complain of a lack of sleep, enthusiasm, and many other ongoing complaints such as all they do is study. Normally, high school students begin their rigorous day at 7 a.m., and end it from 10 p.m. to 1 a.m., which does not make for healthy children. Numerous studies have shown that teens need at least 9 hours sleep to perform well. Yet, here in Korea, the average teen averages 6 hours or less, so it's nothing shy of a miracle that Korean teens learn anything at all! I suppose this is one of the reasons that the U.N declared South Korea in violation of Children's rights?

Article 31

*(1) States Parties recognize **the right of the child to rest and leisure, to engage in play and recreational activities** appropriate to the age of the child and to participate freely in cultural life and the arts.*

*(2) States Parties shall respect and promote **the right of the child to participate fully in cultural and artistic life** and shall encourage the provision of appropriate and **equal opportunities for cultural, artistic, recreational and leisure activity.***

To be fair, not all parents find this in the best interest - mentally or physically – of their children and will allow their children to attend a vocational school, where study is much more humane.

Sadly, the pressure to excel creates an atmosphere of competition between students. In place of academic cooperation, one sees cut-throat competition among peers. This competition is simply far too demanding. Too often, parents place expectations on their children that are simply absurd. These expectations create peer competition.

The current educational system ensures that children from well-off families have the best tutors, thus have access to the top universities. Student achievement, it can be said, correlates with wealth. Students who reject this system often become unmanageable in and outside the classroom.

Finally, many Asian countries use Korea for a base line comparison for cram schools. Singapore's education minister, for example, has stated that his country is not nearly as bad concerning hagwon study as the Koreans. This author believes that China will soon become the country of comparison. To wit, I recently read an article showing Chinese students hooked up to an I.V while at a cram school.

Where will it end, if ever?

Catch 22 Revisited

By now, you should be aware of what a quagmire education is in Korea. If not, let me revisit this debacle using as few words as possible. Parental distrust and dissatisfaction, in part, are what really drive this dysfunctional system. If not for the Tiger Mother, in particular, private academies would cease to exist and we would not have a society in conflict with the educational goals and policies of its government. Therefore, the hagwon culture, be it online or offline, will continue far into the future. In all fairness, I do believe that the government is trying to address issues that drive parents away from public education and to private schools and tutoring, but parents are simply not buying it.

The real conundrum is that the current government policy regarding the rights of parents to educate their children, but at the same time avoiding tutoring that is too expensive, places the burden smack dab on the shoulders of the parents and is asking them to handcuff themselves, and to handicap their children's educational opportunities as well. Truly a damned if you do, damned if you don't scenario. Moreover, Korean society as a whole cannot afford to opt out of the hagwon system. If it did, most of its children would fall through the cracks.

The private education trend challenges "*the time-honored belief that we should have a free education system for equity,*" as said by former President Lee. Families who are "*paying for something value it differently,*" and as parents invest more heavily in the private sector, "*they let public schools abdicate their role as an education provider,*" he further stated.

Indeed, Tiger Mothers are what give impetus to the Korean educational quagmire. Just so, high school teachers sometimes display a hint of integrity by suggesting to their students that they avoid hagwons and focus on school content instead. The most common reply is *"my mother won't let me."* The Tigers know that other Tigers are sending *their* children to hagwons, so they are forced to compete with one another. Typically, as stated previously, hagwons teach ahead of public school, so the Tigers suffer profound anxiety if they allow their children to study at a less stressful rate than others.

I recently read a study posted on the Korea Educational Development Institute website which stated the changes in Korean private education expenses from 1990 to 2010 and also forecasted the amount of private education expenses for the next five years, from 2011 to 2015. On the one hand, the survey found that the *nominal regular* education expenses have increased annually by an average of 5.8 percent, and *actual regular* education expenses have decreased annually by an average of 0.3 percent. On the other hand, the survey also found that *nominal* private education expenses and *actual* private education expenses have both increased by an average of 12.5 and 5.5 percent, respectively.

What this means is that Korean parents must shoulder higher expenses for private education going forward. The study also found that, with regard to the changes based on income levels, the gap between *regular* education expenses among income levels has increased, though in comparison to the ordinary income, regular education expenses have decreased for the ordinary income level. However, *private* education expenses at all income levels have gradually increased, as has the gap between income levels. Specifically, the household burden for private education has dramatically increased for middle and upper income levels. The forecast for private education expenditure for the next five years shows that *nominal* private education expenses are expected to increase by an average of 0.6% percent per quarter for the next five years, while *actual* private education expenses will decrease by an average of 0.3 percent per quarter. Put simply, the amount of private education expenses for the next five years will increase at a relatively decreased rate, and thus the actual household burden for private education will decrease slightly.

Perhaps by now you're beginning to understand the cyclical nature of Korea's educational system. Parents, mostly the Tigers, distrust the public school system, which in turn drives private education. Cognizant of this parental distrust, the Korean Ministry of Education has implemented standardized tests meant to motivate competition among schools and more after-school tutoring at public schools and on TV that are largely cosmetic. Again, parents are not buying it.

Hagwons that take a more humanist approach to teaching English are few and far between. A few brave souls have tried, but have failed. I know of one idealist director who attempted to open a school that emphasized preparing students for globalization. Add to that, he fully realized the futility of memorizing useless vocabulary, so he focused on a more humanist, pragmatic approach – similar to Finland's. Naturally, the Tigers weren't having any of it, and he eventually had to close doors.

This leads us to the second driver of demand for the hagwon culture. Tigers know well that a big investment in their children's education can lead to entrance to an elite university, as mentioned earlier. Graduation from said elite university can further lead to a very secure future, which is what every Korean Tiger Mother desires. Conversely, Koreans also know that poor performance in secondary and high school may lead to decreased employment opportunities, and to the acceptance of a blue collar position.

24

Yet, despite years of study and preparation for the CSAT, there are no guarantees that students will succeed in gaining entrance to an elite university. Many students attend hagwons for years on end but fail to enter one of the top schools. It's really a crap shoot. Obviously, the system favors those who can afford to hire top tutors for acceptance to a top school. Many Koreans, and this author, simply wish that one day public education would suffice.

And yet one more absurdity: one Korean online hagwon now offers 2-year-olds a 20-minute-per-week tutoring service that includes Korean, basic English, and math!

Personally, I agree with Finland's educational philosophy: teaching and learning focus on deep and broad learning giving equal value to all aspects of an individual's growth of personality, moral, creativity, knowledge and skills. I realize, naturally, that parents must be very involved with their children's education; sometimes even forcefully. Yet, one of the many aspects in which I part ways with the Korean system is that *love and affection should not be sacrificed for grades. Korean parents, particularly the Tiger Mother, almost without fail sacrifice affection for grades, which to this author is unthinkable.*

Chapter 3

Hagwons - Language Institutes and Academies

In One Ear, Out the Other

Language institutes / academies / cram schools (hagwons) are yet another unwritten book, so bear with me while I detail these institutions without having to write a second book. I'm beginning with hagwons for a definitive reason: these institutes are where most of you will begin. First, however, please allow me to throw a few figures your way, so you will come to understand just how serious learning English in a hagwon really is.

Eight of every 10 students from elementary school through high school take after-school classes from private tutors or at cram schools, online and offline. Offline cram school courses cost up to five times as much as their online counterparts.

As you have seen, Tiger Mother's survivalist instincts, public education distrust, and globalization, whether negative or positive, are the architects of this English language fanaticism. With that in mind, I, again, believe it fair to say that English will continue to be of significant value in the future. To wit, as I used to watch new high-rise apartments being constructed around me, I was quick to notice that hagwons were fast to follow. In many cases, they were the first businesses to be constructed in the neighborhood of the new apartments. Some here, myself included, call this the *hogownization* of Korea, which means precisely that. As you've seen, this is a multibillion dollar business. Make no mistake about it.

From my extensive experience in many teaching venues, I have found that English, as studied in Korea, is treated as a subject to be studied, not as a tool for communication or a gateway to a new culture, spirit, ideology and more. I used to ask my middle and high school hagwon students why they wished to study English when I was placing them in levels, and many replied that they needed to achieve better scores. English exams have existed in Korea for decades and test scores were believed to be more important, and still are to a large extent, than English proficiency itself. Yet another explanation, one quite common, is simply that they had to study English because their Tiger Mothers demanded it. Not very good reasons for language learning, I would think.

But I digress. As noted earlier, there are thousands of these institutes in Korea. Indeed, it's not unusual to see from 5 to 10 of them on the same block, depending on how many stories the buildings have. Some hagwons are so large that they occupy 4 or 5 stories of a building. From the 17 floor of my former apartment, I could see nearly 8 English language hagwons.

Regarding enrollment in hagwons, the last figure I was privy is that from 2009: student enrollment in English language hagwons, as reported by the Ministry of Finance was recorded at an astounding 1,871,000 students. This was the number that was reported. Imagine the numbers that were not. This upward trend has and will increase due in part to the former president and his misplaced belief that English language proficiency will lead to instant global success for its practitioners.

As you've seen, Korea is a hagwon nightmare. Why? Korean education, while somewhat improved during the last 10 to 15 years, still has much to be desired; overcrowded classrooms do not allow for attention given to students as individuals. Korean teachers don't teach individuals, they teach the masses. Obviously, students who fall behind have one hell of a time catching up. Enter the hagwon.

Korean parents, depending on their economic standing, spend anywhere from 120,000 won ($130 USD) to thousands on private education for each child each month. One of largest hagwons in Korea reported that the maximum amount of tuition Korean parents were willing to pay for each child was 250,000 won ($230 USD) per month.

All hagwons, however, are not created equal; some are much more expensive than others. Interestingly, this same famous hagwon surveyed parents regarding their plans to continue paying the same fee. They found that 54 percent of them planned to continue, while 37 percent said they would increase spending. Not surprisingly, only 8 percent said they wanted to decrease fees. I think it's fairly reasonable to say that Tiger Mothers believe that more money equals better instruction. In fact, the survey states the same. When asked why they paid high fees, 50 percent of mothers stated that they felt higher fees would lead to better English education. Other answers included not being trained to teach their children at home (25 percent), and they were afraid their children would fall behind the other students (16 percent). OK, Korean Tiger Mothers, yet another black mark against you

In Seoul, for example, there are many hagwons charging fees of 300,000 won (280 USD) per month for English instruction. Some, however, charge even more. Even outside of Seoul, hagwons charge similar fees, not to mention the increasingly expensive textbooks and associated workbooks and CDs.

But it's much more than that; Tiger Mothers in particular, are, and I have a difficult time finding the proper description, fanatical about their children's education. Thus those who have the finances enroll their children in hagwons that teach such subjects as music, art, Korean games, language, Lego - believe it or not - and so on and so forth.

Moreover, due to poor methodology and teacher education, which are slow to improve, parents sometimes simply send their children to hagwons to have taught what is not, but should be, in the public schools. Finally, there are many parents who must work during evening hours and on Saturdays. What better babysitter than a hagwon? Knowing that, is it any wonder that there is such an abundance of hagwons?

Teaching at a hagown will give you an incredible appreciation of having a normal (?) childhood because Korean children rarely do. The good news is that most Korean children are not aware of this fact. Frankly, this has had an enormously negative effect on my marital life. If you harbor notions about marrying into this culture, get prepped for the Tiger Mother. Fight the good fight, I always says.

Qualifications—Can I do it?

While it's still possible to come to Korea with a degree in any subject and be hired, you'll not be hired by a college, university, or corporation/company; but, you will be able to find work at a language institute, English language village, public and private school.

With that in mind, the above will not hire you (legally) if you are not in possession of a valid passport (from an English speaking country); a filled out E-2 class visa application form; a 3 or 4 year an apostilled diploma (from any discipline) from a university located in an official English speaking country; transcripts from an institution, and health and criminal background checks (apostilled).

You may have noticed the parenthesized "*legally.*" There are folks who can, and do, find employment teaching English with no qualifications or documents; aka: "*backpack teachers.*" Under Korean law, such practices are illegal and grounds for deportation and more than a little grief for those who hired the illegal teachers. I'm not going to play god, as much as I would like; just let it be known that you exercise caution and good sense when considering such a scenario.

Along with your undergrad degree, most institutions would really love to see one of the following under your belt: TESOL, Cetla, TESL certificates. The TESL certificates, in particular, are ridiculously easy to obtain these days to the point that more than a few Korean universities offer them. I've also seen many of them offered via online for very little money, indeed. To this teacher, these certificates are presently nothing more than fraud, with the exception of a university certificate.

With that in mind, I'm going to try my best to advise you on obtaining one of these certificates, so you don't waste time and money.

1. A university/college certificate, or most places with a physical address, is preferred.

2. If you're going to study at an institution other than a college, be sure that the institution has a long and stellar history.

3. Do ask about teacher qualifications and make sure they are able to provide evidence of those qualifications.

4. I would avoid all online courses, unless they are offered by an accredited university. To do otherwise is an invitation to fraud.

Private/Franchise Hagwons

I've grouped these two together because, for teachers, at least, there are no major differences. Koreans who believe, somewhat mistakenly, that a hagwon is an instant ticket to wealth open hagwons. I would hazard that 30 percent of these schools close within one year.

Shifts are generally split or block. You will want to choose a hagwon with block shifts. Classes will usually begin at 1:00 p.m. and end at 9:00. To voluntarily choose a split shift over a block shift is sadistic. I recall my first hagwon job was split shift: I began at 8:00 a.m. and ended the shift at 11:00 a.m. I then had to return at 6:00 p.m. and teach until 9:00 p.m. Readers, I have *never* been so tired in my life! I never take naps, but after a week of split shifts, I used to sleep two to three hours every day during my afternoon break. Split shifts are for those who love pain.

It should be mentioned that university language centers are among private hagwons. These language institutes, as they are called, are simply glorified hagwons. You'll be teaching the same target: children and adults.

I would say the major differences are in teacher qualifications, less contact time with children, and no contract nonsense. University language centers tend to hire teachers with graduate degrees, or at least a B.A English/Education. The contact hours are substantially less, and the contract is honored, which is not always the case with some hagwons. Yet another benefit is a much longer vacation; usually four weeks in summer and four weeks in winter. Some university language center teachers also teach credit classes for university students. The downsides are that you will almost always have a split shift—but fewer hours—and you are sometimes lodged in a dorm room on campus.

And absolutely keep one thing in mind: although the huge franchise hagwons are considered *"safer"* than ma and pa hagwons in just about every way, there are many branches of the company, each operating under the umbrella of the home office. So, while the home office may be very reputable, the director of one of the branch hagwons may be much less than reputable. That's why you absolutely must do your homework when you begin your job search.

The Director: No, not the FBI

Now, then, every hagwon has an owner, heretofore known as *"The Director."* Let's get a few facts straight about these people:

- Much of the time they have no teaching experience.
- They are profit oriented business people, with few misconceptions or patience for NSET antics.
- When they do discipline students, they do it lightly.
- Even today, there are directors who cannot speak English, or, if they can, do so at an intermediate level.

Note that these days there a few hagwons owned and operated by Westerners. These are folks that usually have a Korean wife or husband. Naturally, they are a bit more understanding of culturally sensitive issues teachers may have, which might make them more desirable than Korean owned hagwons.

My experience with directors has been varied. I've found that female directors are not as easy going as their male counterparts. I've had some pretty intense battles with women directors who disagreed with my teaching methodology and, in one case, I resigned - contract or no contract. You can't do that, dear reader, so don't try it. Just so, female teachers might consider having a female director, and male teachers, male directors.

The Mothers: The Adjumma Network

What makes or breaks a hagwon? The Ajumma (married woman/homemaker) network. The Ajumma grapevine is particularly pervasive in this country, and not only can they mean the ruin of a hagwon, but of any business!

I've really never seen word-of-mouth so pervasive until I began teaching in Korea. It's absolutely everywhere. Koreans, and I'm not stereotyping, are easily influenced by what others think, do, or say. They will not entertain patronizing a business if, for example, they do not see many cars outside of a restaurant, people in a café, children in a hagwon, or someone else's word that so-and-so is no good; therefore, hagwon directors willingly and graciously cow-tow to the students' mothers. This is unfortunate, but it can be dealt with.

A typical hagwon classroom may consist of anywhere from 4 to 14 students, depending on the size and popularity of the school. Popularity depends a lot on the hagwon's teachers, meaning you, readers, if you choose to accept this venue.

If you wish to survive the hagwon culture, keep in mind a fact of English education in Korea: *Very few Korean students are passionate to learn English. Parents are passionate, students are not.* Ordinarily, the most passionate students are those denied English language instruction from a native speaker – students at rural schools, for example.

The Hidden Actor: Am I Popular?

As previously mentioned, teacher popularity is important. Success as a teacher in Korea, and this applies to most venues, depends on one's ability to entertain. If you have actor/comedian blood coursing through your veins, you'll do well. Honest-to-god, knowledgeable teachers, which are very few in Korea, do have a place, but, alas, it's not in the hagwon, unless they simply wish to work part-time or are offered a ridiculously tempting wage.

My experience in the hagwon setting has run the gamut. Suffice to say, my greatest success as a teacher in the hagwon was in the *free speaking* classes with adults. My greatest failure has been with the children's conversation hour. However, that was then and this is now. I have gained much insight into the art of teaching children since then, so I imagine that I would do much better given the opportunity.

Hagwons typically cater to nearly every age category and occupation imaginable. I've taught every school age and many adults: lawyers, doctors, dentists, professors, and soldiers. But, honestly folks, the target is children. Mothers tend to keep their kids in hagwons much longer than any of the adults, which means more revenue for the director. Adults, for the most part, come and go quite often, so the director won't waste a lot of energy on trying to recruit them.

The Children: Good Cop, Bad Cop?

Children can and will be the most challenging aspect of teaching at a hagwon. If you have little tolerance for children's antics, or are not well-trained in childhood education, scroll down and look for another teaching venue; you will not be successful in the hagwon or you will have one very miserable year. Oh, yes, you may finish your one-year teaching contract, but you will leave Korea with a very negative view of teaching and teaching Koreans in general.

There are many reasons for failure to connect with the kids, but one of the most primary is this: there exists a conception about hagwon teachers among its students; *you are not a REAL teacher.* This conception leads to poor behavior, lack of respect, and will stress a teacher to no end. I discuss this in detail later in the book, so don't melt down yet. Make no mistake, if you're idealistic, you may not find the hagwon gig a rewarding one. Of course, there are exceptions, and some hagwon teachers spend a wonderful year and even re-contract after their year is up. Most, however, begin looking for greener pastures here or elsewhere.

Hagwon directors, and the corresponding headhunters (teacher recruiters) are usually on the lookout for reasonably young, attractive, dynamic people. As an aside, I don't know how many times I've read complaints from a certain racist Korean group about blond hair and blue eyes. What in the hell is up with that? More often than not, however, recruiters will settle for a warm body that speaks English and has the proper qualifications. These days, I'm happy to say, I'm seeing more African Americans come to Korea, which was unheard of in the past. Be aware, however, that you will generate no small amount of attention. Koreans behave well with Caucasians, but beware if your skin color is something other than white. Korea was once called "*The Hermit Kingdom.*" This moniker still applies to many aspects of Korean society.

Now, children, as I've come to know them, can be absolutely delightful little people. I know mine are. Was it

Huxley that said every child is a genius until age ten? Just so, once you bring four or more children together, herd instinct tends to evolve. The first few weeks may sail along just fine as the kids gauge you, and you them. As they become more comfortable around you, they may begin to test you. If one misbehaves, the rest take advantage of it. Classroom management becomes more difficult with each passing week. Whether they do this consciously or not, I still haven't figured out; but I know from experience that this is the way of many Korean children.

There are many hagwon horror stories involving Korean children; however, there are just as many hagwon success stories. If you find yourself in a difficult teaching environment, remain calm; having a K-rage will get you nowhere but a visit with the director in the director's office. Said visit will not be of the pleasant variety, regardless if your K-rage was justified or not. Recall that children are the director's bread and butter, and it will be your job to ensure that the director's bread is well-buttered. To do otherwise just won't cut it. If you're popular with the children, you'll be popular with the director, also.

Beware the Dark Side

With this easing of tension, the kids may quickly become a real pain in the butt. Unless you're a hell of an entertainer, or have experience in childhood education, you'll lose them fast. Try to remember this: 99.9 percent of them *do not* know why they are there. Korean mothers, I believe, try to explain why they must study English, but honestly, readers, Korean Tiger Mothers have their heads up their – well you know what. They simply don't understand that children could care less about careers, second languages, globalization, and explanations far beyond children's maturity level. I will also discuss this in detail a bit later in the book.

My point is, when you apply too much force on children to do something, which every Tiger Mother specializes in, it simply does not make for a motivated child, which in turn makes some children difficult to teach. To that end, if I ever taught in (or owned) a hagwon again, I would use 50 percent film. I never really knew the power of movies as effective language instruction, but these days I do. As a matter of fact, teaching using film might be my next book?

Your job will be teaching conversation, for the most part. Most of the kids, depending on their ages, will already have some reading and writing skills to work with the texts. And, often as not, contact time usually begins after 1:00pm. Energy levels and attitudes run from "*I could care less*" to enormous "*let's rock!*" so don't expect them to be perfectly cooperative little angels. In most cases, it simply doesn't happen that way. Anyone who has taught children, or has children, knows well how exhausting they can be.

Related to that, I don't know how many times I had phoned a child's mother explaining that her child's behavior had become unacceptable. What's salient here is how shocked those mothers were when they heard what their child had been up to. The usual response? "*I guess I don't know my child that well.*" My response? "*Well, now you know.*"

What Is Unacceptable?

- Excessive speaking of Korean in class. Be careful here, I would *never* advocate an English only classroom.
- Talking, laughing, and wrestling with classmates while I'm trying to teach.
- Disrespect and disobedience.

I had a policy in my classes; any of the above three that happened more than three times a month would get the child a phone call to their mother. You will *not* be able to do this, so don't even consider it. I did, but then, I was the boss! Now, then, you're not the boss, but you can keep the three time rule; but instead of the phone call, simply move the child to a chair in the corner, and make him or her wait there until the class is over. Korean teachers also use a pretty effective discipline measure; all the children, it doesn't matter that only one child has misbehaved, must keep their arms raised in the air until the teacher says to drop them. I've used this one and it works pretty well.

I realize that these measures may seem harsh, and they are. I *always* try to reason with children first, rather than dish out punishment haphazardly. And while I'm on the subject, please remember you are not behaviorists; rewarding only correct answers and behavior. Skinner, my friends, was an idiot. And while I'm referring to Skinner, please don't give the kids treats for rewarding good behavior. This leads to all kinds of problems in the days to come. If you must have a reward system, use stars, ink pads with happy faces, etc.

Why do these issues occur? Could it be the mothers? Yes, it's the mothers. Korean mothers allow children a lot of freedom to be unruly while they are young. In so far as the moms are concerned, their children can do no wrong. Most mothers also believe that knowledge of good manners and etiquette are the responsibilities of public school teachers. How absurd is that? My ex-wife, an elementary school teacher, once got a phone call from an upset parent. One of her male students slapped a female student. The girl's father phoned my ex and asked "*What are you teaching your students? It's your job to teach them proper manners.*" Obviously, my ex was none too pleased with this moron of a father. Real education, as any caring parent knows, begins at home.

I have, on rare occasions, had children that were not teachable. By that, I mean uncontrollable. I kept my three time rule and ended up ejecting them from the school. I had to refund the parents' money, but I had no problem with that. Afterward, everything sailed along quite smoothly. You need to remember that uncontrollable children ruin the learning experience for the others. I've had many children tell me privately that they wish so-and-so was not in their class, so they could tell their mothers that they are learning, at the very least, a little. Again, you won't be able to eject them from your class, but you can have a word with the director.

I've taught children as young as five, but generally, your hagwon students will be at least nine (1st grade), which is eight in the West. If you've never taught this age group before, you'll be in for a few adjustments. You'll quickly learn how easily distracted kids can get. Even a pencil becomes an imaginary space ship, a top or a weapon. Thus, it's always best to have around as few distractions on the desks or tables as possible unless they are absolutely necessary. Related to that, you'll come to know how patient and tolerant you are. I've listened to many a teacher exclaim how Buddha-like tolerant they are, only to break down in tears when they've been around a classroom full of Korean nine-year-olds for a while.

Consider this: if you have any of the following personality characteristics, you probably won't want to teach children in Korea: over excitable, melancholy, sarcastic, cynical, frustrated, and over-bearing. If, however, you have the capacity to tune into the minds and feeling of kids, you'll be welcome here and be better equipped to teach children.

Curricula: Textbooks and Other Garbage

I would hazard to guess that 85 percent of hagwons, particularly the franchise hagwons, have set curricula, which includes text choice. I'm by no means a fan of hagwon text choice. There is little worse than teaching a text that is poorly written or downright boring, which includes about 99 percent of them. There are more than a few evils to teaching English, and textbooks are at the top of my list, followed by textbook authors, and textbook publishers.

The students, at some point, will really come to hate the texts, as will you. Just so, if you've been given a lemon, grab the tequila! It's entirely doable to make a mediocre, or worse, text into an acceptable one. I've had to do so more times than I care to admit. Keep in mind that I've taught, at last count, 43 texts, so I know what I'm talking about.

Many of the larger franchise hagwons have in-house texts that cover the gamut of language learning, or work hand in glove with textbook publishers. The texts are designed to milk as much money as possible from the students' parents. I was once graced with having to teach phonics to my students using in-house texts. My god, I thought the texts would never end! Six textbooks, folks! The books that I ordinarily teach have no more than 3 and do the job much better. Most of the in-house text's quality ranges from poor to a very serious waste of paper. However, you'll have no choice; you must teach the texts that you are given.

Despite set curricula, teachers may still have a bit of freedom to choose which activity – if any - they will use after the lesson; usually a board or card game. Here's yet another pearl of wisdom: you can *never* have too many games in your arsenal. Remember, you'll be seeing most of your students five days a week, so you've got to have variety. Variety, readers, is one of the key ingredients to success in the classroom. Variety extends to games, in particular. Most hagwons will have a good collection of games, but, just so, the classics are always good to go with: Go fish, Crazy Eights, Old Maid, Bingo language games, of which there are many varieties, are good for a few months before the kids burn out. Junior Scrabble is good for nearly a year, if not played too often. It's a good game for teaching alphabet recognition and pronunciation. Junior Monopoly is an all-time favorite, but it usually takes too much time. However, if you dedicate the entire hour to it, you'll be okay. Consonant Blends and Digraphs is a great game for teaching phonics. You can also break out the classics: Hangman, Pictionary. Be warned, however, that the game thing can really get out of hand quickly. The kids will not want to concentrate; they will rush through the day's lesson so they can get to the good stuff: games. With that in mind, I used to limit games to Friday, only.

If, by some luck, you find yourself free to choose your own curricula, have the director buy three or four texts: speaking, listening, reading comprehension, language arts, and cycle them one per class. Variety, remember, is of utmost importance.

In the Classroom: Am I Still Breathing?

One of the things I learned early on was to pace myself. Remember, you'll have from five to eight 40 or 50-minute lessons per day. Even if you don't have split shifts, you will tire because if you're teaching elementary school children, you'll be on your feet a lot. Other age groups, bless their hearts, will allow you to sit while teaching.

You've got to be dynamic with children; to do otherwise just won't cut it. Get off your feet and sing and dance and have a blast at least a few times a week. You've got to put them to work physically, so they can let loose some of that pent-up energy. I should mention, however, that when you teach after 7:00pm that the kids are sometimes pretty drained and uncooperative. This, as noted earlier, is because they've already been to three or four other hagwons. The afternoon hours, though, are an entirely different ball game; they'll still have some get up and go.

I don't know about you, but my legs get a bit worn out after three hours of standing and moving around. As an aside, when I think of all the coffee I used to drink to keep energized, it's a wonder I didn't jettison through the ceiling. Try to balance your energy output, so you don't burn out too early in the game. Take advantage of your class breaks to relax and get psyched for the next round.

Dress: To Vagabond or Not

To say that Koreans place a lot of importance on appearance would be a gross understatement. Even construction laborers dress reasonably well. When I was in the hagwon, ownership notwithstanding, I dressed casually. Three seasons of the year meant blue jeans and a nice shirt, and during the summer a nice pair of knee-length shorts and a T-shirt. Fast forward to today and I have found little change in hagwon dress. I even see this same attire at the local university language institute, which I find a little surprising.

Women wear basically the same attire as above. In fact, I can't remember the last time I saw a dress or skirt on a Western woman. That doesn't mean that you can't dress well. I do, but then my clients are professionals, so it helps that I look professional, also. I also dress well when I have university classes, just as I should. However, if I found myself in the hagwon again, I would return to casual attire.

You must also keep in mind that your classroom may not have a good source of heat in the winter. My classrooms had portable LPG heaters, which were infinitely better than the kerosene heaters of old. Just so, they were slow to heat the classrooms in the morning, so I dressed for the cold. Conversely, during the summer you don't have to concern yourself with a hellish classroom because all hagwons now have AC. The entire hagwon, in fact, will have AC.

Outdoors is an entirely different matter. The summer months are unbearably hot and humid, while the winters are bone-chilling cold, so dress accordingly and don't worry about looking fashionable; to hell with that.

Party, Party. Did I Say Party? Outside the Hagwon

If I had a dollar for every teacher I've seen burnout from partying on a school night, I do believe I could buy another new car. It's very common, particularly among new teachers, to go downtown after classes. They used to call this *"chicken night"* back in the day. Many teachers from different hagwons would get together at a fried chicken restaurant/pub, and proceed to get wasted, which is okay if you finish classes early; you can drink a bit, go home and still get a decent night's rest. The caveat is that most classes finish at 9:00 or 10:00, so you won't have a lot of time.

I've never attended these meetings. However, I've known a few who have. I've been told that these meetings often turn out to be nothing more than bitch and moan sessions about students, directors, co-teachers, and Koreans in general. I don't need all of that negativity. My sons are bi-cultural, so to hell with that.

It's much easier on your health if you find yourself moderately isolated. Small cities simply don't have the NSET population compared to large cities, so you may not be as tempted to become the party animal. You may also make some life-time friends, Korean and foreign. The city where I live has a population of 250,000 folks. The average amount of English teachers in this size of city is roughly 40 to 60. Smaller communities, say less than 100,000, have around 10 to 20 teachers.

Teaching adults can be a lot of fun. As stated earlier, my greatest success has been with the adult classes. I quickly became the most popular teacher in the university hagwon district due to my methodology and wit. This was in the free speaking classes. The other adult classes, which were conversation based, were also very nice. My education and background are in linguistics, so I found the many opportunities to really improve students' English, particularly with prosody and phonetics.

You may be asked to accompany the adult students to a pub or restaurant after you've finished teaching for the day. I *always* accepted, as it gave them the chance to use English in real time. Your director will also love you for this, for obvious reasons. Remember to use moderation if you begin drinking alcohol. Teaching children, or anyone for that matter, with a hangover is not my idea of fun.

Choosing the Right Hagwon: The Journey Begins

Never, and I can't stress this enough, accept a job advertised by a recruiter unless you have a personal relationship or the recruiter comes highly recommended from people you trust with your life. If you're not familiar with the term, headhunters are teacher recruiters. Most do not care who you are, so long as you breathe and speak English – any English. If any recruiters are reading this and disagree, this onus is on you to prove differently, folks, not me. Now let's run through a possible job search routine.

A good number to begin with would be around 5 possible positions.

- Print out the job listings
- Prioritize those jobs beginning with number 1
- Make notes on the margins noting why you like the listing. My priorities were:
  a. private lodging
  b. contact hours
  c. salary
  d. vacation

Begin your research with job one. Most listings will give you a contact phone number or an email address, which may belong to the director or a current NSET at the school. If the contact phone number turns out to be the director's, well, you will want to ask if you can speak with a current teacher - a former teacher is desirable, but not always possible - regarding the teaching position. You'll want to ask the teacher if he or she has a home phone number where they can be reached. What you don't want to do is begin asking questions of the teacher with the director in the same room, obviously.

Okay, you've made contact with the teacher. Below are the questions you will want to ask about each possible job opening.

Oh, yes, don't be afraid to get down and dirty. It's *your* future.

- Ask about the positive/negatives of the school.
- Ask about the students – negatively or positively motivated, (naturally, much of that depends on the teacher) and their ages.
- The director and whether he/she will back you up you should need to discipline students. How personable is the director and at what level is his/her English.
- Split shifts, begin in the morning, have lunch and return in the afternoon, or block shifts, begin in the morning, finish in the afternoon, or begin in the afternoon and finish in the evening. Give me block shifts any day. It's nice to get it over with, so you can relax later.
- Lodging. Some genuine nightmares here, readers. Some unscrupulous directors have been known to put teachers in apartments that are barely habitable. Be very careful with this one. It's highly desirable to get a few photographs of the apartment where you will be lodged. Related to that, ask whether or not your lodging will be private or whether you have to share with other teachers. Moreover, find out how far away your lodging is from your school. If you wish to work in a large city, you may be in for long commutes.
- Teaching methodology. Are you free to design your own curricula and choose the texts, or must you follow school policy.
- Wages. This one is of major importance. Directors often cheat teachers of their salary, pay late, or not pay at all. Get the low-down on this one, particularly. Make sure the director pays on time, every time. You will also want to

know exactly how much your wage will be after all deductions have been accounted for, which include taxes, pension and health insurance deductions.

- Have the director or contact teacher fax, text, or email you a copy of the contract so you can look it over, no matter if you're overseas or in Korea, and then read the chapter on contracts in this book.

- Teaching contact hours. Ninety five percent of hagwons demand that teachers teach at least 30 hours a week. Whew! Get used to it. In addition, get a precise number for how many classes you will be required to teach each day, as well as when you are required to be at the hagwon, how long each class is, and whether or not you are given a short break between each class.

- Will the hagwon farm you out? Many hagwons send their teachers to teach at companies, schools, and god knows where. This is a major burden on teachers and if you find the hagwon does indeed farm teachers out, you may want to walk away from it. I do know a few teachers working for the Korean YMCA who are farmed out, but they don't seem to mind it too much. Their duties are teaching a few hours a day at various public elementary schools. One teacher I know, in particular, was even given a car to commute to his various classes. Nice. If you can, try to score a job like YMCA that will farm you out humanely. It's much less stressful.

- Vacation time. Ordinarily, you'll be allowed two weeks; one week in summer and one in winter. You will also have all holidays off. Be sure you establish just when you are allowed to take your vacation time, and that your vacation time *does not* include national holidays

- If you're overseas, will the hagwon pay for your flight ticket to Korea? Used to be very rare, but it's becoming more common these days.
- How much money is deducted from your check for pension and health insurance? You have no choice on this one, readers. Every teaching venue in Korea deducts for pension and health insurance. You will receive your pension at the end of your contract, so relax.
- Class load. How many students on average for each class. More is *not* better. Directors are notorious for overpopulating a class, which severely limits teacher effectiveness and creates some major classroom management problems. I suggest no more than eight students per class, which is too many for this teacher. I used to limit classes to four, so I could keep an eye on them. Caveat: schools with four or less students per class may be experiencing financial distress, so beware of that before signing.
- Many hagwons will give you the equivalent of one month's salary as a bonus if you teach for the contract's duration. Ask about this one
- Is there a monthly wage increase for re-contracting? Yes, readers, some hagwons will up your wage if you re-contract
- Precisely what day are you to be in Korea? Yes, I know, the contract states the first contact day, but no mention is made of when you must be in Korea. Many hagwons require NSETs to be in

Korea well before the first day of teaching, so make damn sure you know what's what.

- What's the average retention rate for teachers? Some NSETs actually re-contract, believe it not, which may be a positive indicator of the school's quality
- Remember: *much of the above is negotiable.*

Can you trust the contact teacher? Usually, yes, you can. They have little to gain by lying, so while their words are not written in stone, they are fairly reliable. Keep in mind that if you do decide to use a recruiter that the contact person will absolutely *abhor* your questions; thus, they may not respond to your queries regarding a job opening. This is a huge red flag; run, don't walk, away from the job. If by some oddity a recruiter does respond, you may have the opportunity to survive a hagwon job.

Sample teaching advertisement. The real deal.

Here we have a sample teaching ad placed by a hagwon taken from a very popular teaching forum. Let's have a look at it, and see if it suits our demanding criteria for a job. My comments are in **bold** after each point.

Job offer from the beautiful coastal city - Sokcho, Apply now!
Posted By: Jims School example@sample.com
Date: Wednesday, 31 November 2012, at 11:33 a.m.
* Benefit and Working Conditions
- Location: Sokcho, Gangwon province
- Starting date: June, 2012
- Schedule: Monday ~ Thursday (just 4 days) ---**Great! 4 day work week. Very rare.**
- Working Hours: No more than 21 hours a week (starting time 3;00 pm) ---**Again, very rare. This is quickly becoming a quality hagwon!**
- Salary: 1.9 ~ 2.0 million won ---**This is a decent salary for a reduced work week**
- Teaching target: Elementary/ Middle School ---**No surprises here**
- Required Qualifications: Bachelor's Degree ---**Industry standard**
- Housing: Furnished single apartment (5~10 minute walk from the school) ---**The short walk to school makes this one desirable.**
- Vacation: 10 days paid vacation a year + all national holidays ---**Industry standard.**
- Airfare: Round trip ---**Very nice, indeed.**
- National Pension Plan/ Health insurance: 50% paid by the school ---**Industry standard**
- Severance: Equal to one month salary -**Industry standard**
* About Jims School

- Jims School is a small English academy in Sokcho city that has been operating for about 8 years. We are small compared to big franchised institutes but have gained a reputation of quality and friendly instruction here. We limit the maximum number of the students on a class and try to provide a learning-friendly environment for both students and teachers.

* About Sokcho

- Sokcho is a city in Gangwon-do province, South Korea. The city still attracts many national and international tourists, not only because of Seorak-san, but also because of its fine fishery products. The beach of Sokcho has a good reputation although it is only open for 42 days every year. There are natural hot springs in Sokcho, some of which have been developed into spas and pleasure swimming halls. There are also golf courses which are popular because of their natural surroundings.(from Wikipedia) If you are into outdoor activities like hiking, wind-surfing and climbing, this place is for you.

* Contact

- If you have any questions or would like to apply, please contact us by email with your resume and a photograph.

It's obvious that this is a very desirable job. However, it requires one hell of a lot of follow up. You'll want to go through our list and follow up on those points that are not covered in the ad. Best way to do that is to email the director and get the phone number of a current teacher at the hagwon. If the director refuses, walk away; there are hundreds more to choose from.

Now let's look at a more "normal" hagwon position:

Teachers Needed for October Start in Jeju Island, Korea
Posted By: Biffs Academy biff@remail.bot
Date: Thursday, 11 November 2012, at 12:41 p.m.
*Biff's Academy, Jeju: Apply direct to the school. -Biff's Academy on Jeju Island is currently hiring for October.
-Successful applicants will have a genuine affinity for children, a good work ethic and a commitment to education. Experience teaching English to children in Korea is beneficial but not essential.
*Terms and conditions:
-Teaching kindergarten and elementary school students ---**There's the "K" word-kindergarten. You had better love children.**
-2.0 – 2.2 million Won per month based on experience - --**Industry Standard**
-Maximum of 30 hours per week --- **Industry Standard**
-10 vacation days, plus national holidays --- **Industry Standard**
-Monday to Friday, no split shifts ---**Finally, something positive**
-Severance pay upon completion of one-year contract--- **Industry Standard. Inquire about the amount of S. Pay**
-50% medical insurance --- **Industry Standard**
-Round-trip airfare provided from point of hire--- **Industry Standard**
-Furnished apartment provided --- **Industry Standard**

> *Qualifications:
>
> -Native speaker, 4-year university degree (must be able to produce a notarized photocopy of diploma with attached apostille certificate, as well as official transcripts in a sealed envelope for visa processing). If this opportunity interests you, please respond with a cover letter and resume via e-mail to biff@remail If sending attachments, please specify in the subject line that it is an application for Jeff's Academy. All qualified applicants will receive a response within ten days of application

The above ad blankets about 90 percent of all hagwon positions. Again, only a minimum amount of information is given, so follow up is needed.

I should probably mention that your introduction to teaching may well be out of the pot and into the fire. The big franchise schools sometimes do from three to seven days teacher training prior to contact time. The smaller schools usually have no training, so you're on your own and, in many cases, you're on your own in a hell of a hurry. I know more than a few teachers who began teaching a few hours after arriving in Korea. How's that for an intro? Be sure to ask the powers that be whether you'll have training or not, precisely when you will begin to teach your first class, and precisely *what* your responsibilities as a teacher will be.

Breaking the Contract

I've done it (legally); you may have to. I'm aware that this is intended for those already teaching in Korea, but since you may be joining us, I would like you to be as well-informed as possible before you make a decision. I don't condone breaking contracts, but sometimes shit happens and you find yourself up the river without a paddle. This is no laughing matter, so I suggest that prior to breaking the contract that you contact me and discuss alternatives. I will also point you in the right direction regarding contract law, questions, and solutions.

There are, and will continue to be, teachers that break their contracts without first discussing it with anyone. They prepare in advance for a very quick departure from Korea. We here in Korea call this *"The Run."* The definition of the *run* is pretty self-explanatory: leave Korea ASAP. The results of breaking your contract are unpleasant, as you may well have guessed. You'll lose out on money owed you, which may be quite substantial. There used to be rumors floating around that you would be blacklisted and not able to return to Korea after the run. Many runners flatly deny these rumors, and they should know, they've returned to Korea after making the run. I was able to break the contract twice and stay in Korea because I was married to a Korean national. My first incident was with a government run program and the second a hagwon.

I've known a few teachers who have resorted to the run; but, again, I don't condone it. These days, teachers do have legal recourses, so I suggest using those recourses rather than doing the run. I'm not going to go into precisely how to go about doing the run because you can do an internet search and find all the info you need on a few dubious internet websites.

Related to that, be sure to bring at least $1000 USD as a precaution because it may well be five or six weeks before you are paid.

Chapter 4

EPIK: English Program in Korea

A s stated earlier in the book, I came to Korea with a one year contract to teach in the *Korreta* program, now known as EPIK. I had to jump through a few hoops to land the job, but it seemed worthwhile, and it got the good old thumbs up from my ex, who shooed me away from everything else.

Looking back, I've really never seen such a calamity of humanity gathered together in one place. But I won't bore you that. Suffice to say that about 10 out of 600 teachers (?) were there to do the job, the rest...I'm still not sure why they were hired, but my guess is that the program officials were desperate, indeed. *"Hey, can you breathe? You're hired!"*

EPIK, regardless if you've already taught for them, requires a two week training period at KNUE - Korea National University of Education in Cheongju. While not wholly unpleasant, most of it is not very helpful. However, that is the EPIK way, and you are not going to change it.

During your stay at KNUE, you'll be lodged in a dorm room with another trainee. You'll have classes which usually begin after breakfast and continue on through 3:00 or 4:00pm, with timeout for lunch. Lecturers for these classes are usually current or former EPIK teachers, who will attempt to fill you in on what to expect from the program, the students, and co-teachers. However, there will be many other lecturers as well.

Highlight of the whole damn training program was hopping on a very comfortable bus for a three day tour of the country. During that tour, we stopped at a few schools to see how things were done, stayed in some swank hotels, and ate wonderful meals. This highlight has since been dropped from the program, I regret to say, thanks to the boneheads at EPIK

After the training period, you'll have a choice of where you want to teach in Korea. In my day, many chose Seoul, which now has its own English teaching program (administered by EPIK), and very few chose to go to Busan, which was the other choice. These days, you'll have many choices where you would like to teach, and, that, my friends, is a wonderful change.

Now then, listen up. Seoul and Busan are fine, but they tend to wear one down physically and mentally. Much of the time, your lodging will not be near the school where you teach, meaning that you may have a very lengthy subway or bus ride to and from school, which is fine if you're used to such a thing, or you have an astounding tolerance for it. I didn't. My ex made me choose Seoul because she had friends there, so Seoul it was. And, sure enough, lodging was a 35-minute subway ride from the school. I learned to hate the subway and the masses that formed there.

Busan, while metropolitan, does not have the extensive network of subway lines that Seoul has, which could mean an even longer bus ride. However, there have been reports that teachers' lodgings are closer to the schools in Busan than in Seoul. In the smaller cities, lodging is almost always a 10 or 15 minute walk to the school, which adds greatly to a positive experience here. Also, Seoul is simply an enormous furnace in the summer and a freezer in the winter. It has all of the ills of mega-cities everywhere.

Where you teach is decided on a first-come, first-served basis. The desk-warmers at EPIK decide which POE you will be placed at after reviewing your documents. Next, the POE will decide which school you will teach at. You may be placed at an elementary, secondary, or high school. However, many NSETs will also be farmed out to other schools within the POE's umbrella.

Below is a map of the provinces and the largest cities in most of them.

Let's return to my school for a moment. The school was old, the principal a grossly overweight woman of about 50 or 55, who spoke no English and would not look at me when speaking about me. However, the vice-principal was better mannered and personable, so all was not entirely negative. I did, just the same, have the feeling that I was a fish about to be fried. Not a good way to begin a teaching job, folks.

What I remember most about that ordeal were the four KETs overwhelming me with requests in intermediate level

English during my sudden introduction to the school. Nothing in my training, obviously, had prepared me for that. I was told by those KETs to prep about 100 English texts for teaching the following day for thousands of grades (or so it seemed) and have them ready to go the next day! You can imagine my surprise at that. My first thoughts were to hell with that and to hell with you. But much to my relief, one of the KETs was a younger man who seemed to understand my predicament; he took me aside and tried to calm me down and explain just what was expected of me.

These days, conditions are much better. Most schools will go out of their way to welcome you and make sure that you have everything you need; a long way from the beginning of the program. Long story short, I made it through the year. When asked whether I intended to re-contract, I stated that I had contracted with a university, and said my good-bye. Parting with that school was an enormous burden lifted.

Okay, enough back-grounding; let's talk about what it's like in the trenches.

OOOOOOO and AHHHHHHH: Huh?

Your first month in the public school classroom will not be entirely smooth sailing, obviously. You'll be co-teaching with Korean nationals, whose English skills may be quite questionable. Your audience may include elementary, middle, and high school students, depending on which school you've been sent to. Also, keep in mind that your KET might suddenly be feeling lazy, kick back, and let you teach the entire lesson yourself. This absolutely does happen, despite the fact that EPIK guidelines state that a Korean teacher must *always be in the classroom*. The reality, sadly, is much different in many cases.

I've spoken with more than one NSET about this issue and it was the number one complaint among them. When asked why they don't attend the NSETs classes, KETs answers ranged from, *"It's the NSETs' class, so it's their problem"* to *"because I can do other work or take a break."* Many also stated that they were just too busy with their own classes to share teaching responsibility, despite the fact that NSETs are *teaching assistants.* One NSET told me what a huge waste of time and money it was to have NSETs in the Korean classrooms. He, and many others, lack the necessary language skills to properly manage Korean children. When he does try, the students simply don't listen, or laugh at his less than perfect Korean speech. And, yes, this also happened to me to when I taught in this venue. You may want to bear in mind that classroom management should *not entirely* be the NSETs responsibility.

Typically, there will be only a handful of students interested in English; mostly out of curiosity. As usual, they will be seated in the front. Behind them, all manner of behavior takes place: sleeping, talking, holding open conversations, and walking around the room. Even with these less than desired behaviors, I can't remember ever having a K-rage (Korea rage) with a student. However, I do recall coming very near to it more than once. Those were the times in which my KET left the room to do god knows what. All at once, my students went from reasonably attentive to unreasonably uncooperative. In these situations, as a newbie, there really wasn't much I could do but roll with it until my KET returned, which is what I did. I simply desk-warmed until she returned, shocked to find the class in such disarray. I had a face-to-face with her after class, and she guaranteed me that she wouldn't leave the room again. I'm just so overwhelmingly happy that there were no cell/smart phones to put up with back in the day. I would probably go into K-rage mode in a hurry.

Complaints to the school's principal largely fall on deaf ears. POE admins might force the KET back in the class, but after a short while, NSETs again find themselves teaching the class alone. Not only is this detrimental to the NSET, but to the students, also. Related to that, many children have stated that the NSET's class is terrible; too much noise and sleeping, and continual complaints about the class not being interesting or fun.

Seoul education officials are aware of these issues, as are other POEs scattered across Korea. While some justify this as a reason for underfunding or eliminating English Language programs (Seoul Metropolitan Office of Education) others see it as a system that needs fixing. I read that the Ministry of Education, Science, and Technology has invested 309,459,660,000 won (272,663,694.436 USD) in the employment and *management* of NSETs. They have come to realize that NSETs must have KET support in the classroom to maintain discipline and maximize learning. It all makes dollars and sense.

In reality, you'll find that you'll sometimes be teaching the same texts as the KETs, trying to maintain the same rate as them. Typically, KETs should be focused on grammar and vocabulary translations and, you, oh dear potential NSET reader, should focus on speaking and listening skills using that same grammar/vocabulary. Most KETs will not actually make lesson plans with NSETs because they're simply too busy or too lazy to do so. Some will, however, let you know the format they want to use, so you'll not be completely in the dark. This formula works pretty well, all things considered. Just make your exercises fun and interesting as you possibly can; but beware that fun, in a Western cultural sense, does not always translate well here in Korea.

Your KETs will probably be aware that you are not fully qualified in the same sense that they are, so this may lead to disrespect and uncooperative behavior of the KET. Most will see you as a distraction for the students, or, at worst, a novelty. The students might also understand that you are not a *real* teacher, so this aspect may lead to uncooperative behavior. The students know that NSETs do not have the same power as the KETs, so they will often exploit this newly found awareness to their advantage.

Also bear in mind that KETs come in all varieties of behavior and attitude. Regardless, you've got to really try to work with your KETs and attempt to understand their attitudes if you wish to create a reasonably stress-free teaching environment. While some KETs are effective and fun, others are reluctant and stressed. Also remember that your KETs are your liaison with the principal and vice principal. If you have an issue, it's your KET's responsibility to take it to the desk warmers. NSET access to the bureaucracy is indeed rare, so this is yet another reason to have a good relationship with your KETs.

Lack of contact time also seems to be a major problem with teaching in the public school these days. EPIK NSETs often complain that there simply isn't enough of it for students to learn an entire chapter, not to mention retention and reinforcement of the material in that chapter. Many NSETs spend too much time on vocabulary and sentences, so lack of time is really moot. Time should be spent practicing authentic language in authentic contexts and not garbage like "*Happy Birthday*" or "*My pleasure.*"

I suppose, really, that a lot of the blame lies in the texts NSETs must teach. Please recall my diatribe about textbooks in the chapter on hagwons. I believe that public school texts are even worse. To this day, I have not seen a

Korean authored English textbook that is worth the paper it's printed on.

Also, those of us who have learned a second or foreign language know well that three hours of instruction is clearly not enough to learn a language in any meaningful way.

Again, as mentioned in the first chapter, that's precisely why there are so many language hagwons. Students fall behind and once behind, there is no catching up, unless they attend a hagwon.

Indeed, if the Korean Ministry of Education were as serious as they would like to be about English language learning, they might want to increase instruction to 5 hours a week and give NSETs more responsibility, rather than treating English as the least important class in the school. Back in '96, things were so much worse, so certain aspects of language instruction have improved dramatically.

Let's discuss the subtitle of this chapter (finally.) The first time I entered the classroom with my KET, the students in my first class, which were fifth-graders, made a sound something like ooooooowaaaaaaa - a sound that you'll get used to among not only that age group, but older students as well. It's a Korean thing. You'll hear them make this sound when they see or hear something surprising or something or someone they like. After the initial shock wears off, which usually takes only a short time, the more adventuresome students – usually the boys – begin to participate. But remember, in my day native speakers were still somewhat of a novelty, unlike these days. Middle school girls, with few exceptions, were another story; some were far too shy in the presence of a male teacher to participate. I actually had a few of them hide behind their desks when I approached them, which made me roll my eyes and sigh.

Of all grade levels, I prefer the elementary grades most. Students still have a bit of childishness left in them, so they can be reasonably fun to teach. Secondary school is where students are becoming aware of themselves and the opposite sex. High school is where they exploit that awareness. The girls go to great pains to have the perfect look. Just so, high school is not the place for lipstick, perms, curled eyelashes; the system does not allow these, but that doesn't stop the girls from trying.

The texts at that time were in soft cover book form and were odds and ends of exercises thrown together by Korean authors. They were a conglomeration of whatever the authors thought necessary for their target; no rhyme, reason or syllabus behind them. Fast forward to 2013, and I'm finding that, sadly, not much has changed.

The grade schools are big on reading, writing, and grammar, so the texts tend to reflect those aspects of language learning. Class instruction is usually robotic and audio-lingual (drill and kill) methodology is still very much alive. KETs do take seminars that teach other methodologies, communicative in particular. But because class sizes are so large, it's difficult for KETs to use what they've learned, even if they pair up students. Now, then, communicative methodologies are fine in a small class setting but are not so fine in classes of over 30 students. Just so, certain aspects of the communicative technique can be used in larger classes. It just takes a little experimentation. I've dealt with large classes more often than not, so I'll clue you in on how to handle them a bit later.

Because conversation was so badly neglected in the past, Koreans have a devil of a time expressing themselves in English. When they do, their English, naturally, presents every kind of error/mistake imaginable. Korean teachers don't have time, or don't feel comfortable, teaching language aspects such as suprasegmentals (prosody) so most Korean speakers have absolutely no idea what rhythm, stress, and intonation involve. English is predominantly a stress-timed language, but 101 percent of Korean English speakers still speak with syllable-timing, reflecting Korean language prosody. Well, readers, that's one of the reasons the EPIK program is in place - to give Korean school age children the opportunity to use what they've learned in real time with a native speaker. That doesn't mean you'll be teaching prosody directly; you can't unless you have some linguistics classes under your belt.

Furthermore, your KET, who you are supposed to be assisting, will probably not allow it. However, you will be teaching prosody indirectly by virtue of your native speaker status.

Keep in mind that the goal in the public schools is not accuracy, but rather fluency. Unlike a hagwon setting, where class size allows you to work with individuals and their corresponding issues, the public schools won't allow for this. But I'll address that later in the book in the chapter on teaching children.

As a suggestion, you may want to begin with - if your text doesn't introduce it, classroom English, just as I did when I was an NSET. Teach page numbers, student numbers, TPR commands such *as sit down, stand up, come here, put your hands on your head, open your book, close your book, put your things in your desk, get out your scissors, cut out the cards, let's play a game*, and recycle them each class.

This will greatly reduce the need for your KET to translate. Keep in mind the level which you're teaching; each level will have different needs. At the elementary level, you can introduce creativity into your lessons by prepping the text for humor. I should say, I added to the text what I thought would be humorous questions. To this day, I still use many humorous {WH} questions. Much to my satisfaction, that was the key to retaining their attention. Also, if you use language compensation, your students will understand you, for the most part. I used to think of it as *"dumbing down,"* but I learned that I was simply compensating for the learner's level; and that, my friends, is one very important key to success in the classroom. Keep it simple. Keep it *very* simple.

At other levels, though, beware; students tend not to have much (any) experience with creative activities. You can be a creative monster only to have your activities totally bomb,

66

so don't come unglued when that happens; it's not your fault, it's the system's fault. At the higher grades, focus is very much on exams, scores, points, which does not make for creatively enlightened students.

It's all thinking inside the box. Once you come to realize this, you'll be better positioned to either challenge it, or go with it.

That doesn't mean you shouldn't try to be creative; just beware. So what does work? The mundane, sadly. Structured exercises such as drill and kill, worksheets of nearly any kind, word searches, etc. The more bored you are, the more excited they are.

What you'll find in the public schools are Korean teachers who tend to keep a pretty tight rein on students' behavior. Remember, readers, teachers here once enjoyed the freedom to hand out serious corporal punishment, and it was not very long ago that it was deemed unacceptable by the Korean people and government, although it is still *not* considered illegal. Nevertheless, Korean teachers don't tolerate student B.S very well. My ex teaches second graders this year, and I know she absolutely will not tolerate any student antics (Tiger teacher.) The point that I'm trying to make is that you'll have a pretty easy time of it regarding student management. Caveat: bear in mind that much of your success depends on your KET. Some are inexcusably lazy while others simply don't like to cooperate with an NSET, despite what the contract states. Many NSETS complain that the KET is only good for classroom management and little else, which was fine by me. Mind you, you'll want to establish who is going to lead the class long before actual contact time. If you do so, your KET may be more motivated to participate in creative activities.

Fortunately for me, I did not experience the "*us vs. them*" mentality that so many NSETs and KETs experience these days. I was able to communicate, albeit not without many problems, with my KETs, and I got along with them quite well. However, the program was in its infancy, so we simply did not know what to expect of each other for the first few months. Eventually, we were able to iron out many of the co-teaching wrinkles that did arise. I recall one KET in particular that simply wanted to dominate the class each and every time we co-taught. But, after discussing this problem with her in a rational manner, she agreed to my suggestions. You may not be so fortunate, you may have KETs that have the attitude that you are not a real teacher (I personally have yet to find more than a handful of *genuinely* professional Korean teachers); ergo no respect, no communication other than texts or email, and no real cooperation. Be ready for confrontation.

If you simply can't get through to your KET, have him/her do classroom management while you teach. Some KETs will simply refuse all requests. To be fair to the KETs, these government English teaching programs were not their idea. Many are forced to co-teach, and they are not happy about it. Just so, the ways in which KETs display this unhappiness are neither professional nor mature.

You need to remember *why* you are in the classroom; you are a native speaker of English, so go with your skills. You teach the dialogues, listening, songs and, if you are fortunate to have a cooperative KET, have him/her teach reading – most KETs can *read* English – and game time.

Most of my co-teachers, when they finally learned to relax when speaking with me, were okay. Again, their English skills were questionable, but that's why they relied so heavily on the text. What became particularly bothersome was when they asked me to tutor them – for free. Normally, I would never accept such a proposal. But under the circumstances, what choice did I have? It seemed my principal was also behind the idea, so I found myself doing extra work within one month. These days, I believe that you may have a choice as to whether or not you want to take on extra work. If you do, you'll be compensated for it.

One of the current contractual issues is one in which many schools have educational policies that supersede the EPIK contract. If you complain to your school's principal or vice principal that your contract is being superseded, you will most likely be told that you have no choice. Each school has its own policies, and most principals will not negotiate with you, even if you do have access to them. This is engrained in Far Eastern cultures; the collective is more important than the individual. The greater good is all that is important. You absolutely must be aware of this cultural norm, because it occurs quite often.

You'll not have an office of your own; they exist only for the top echelon of the school. No, you'll have a desk in the teachers room; thus, no privacy. If you were born under a good sign, you might have a desk in the English language classroom, which is preferable, obviously. However, not every school, particularly small rural schools, has a room dedicated to English and English, only. This is a major hassle because if you wish to decorate your classroom with English media, you simply can't. Related to that, it is really rare to find a school that has teaching realia at the ready. Materials such as large flash cards, scissors, paste, teaching supplements, and construction paper just don't exist, so you'll have to deal that, also.

During each semester, you'll have to give a teaching demonstration, which is mostly for students' parents. The demonstration is a monstrous waste of time because it is so well-rehearsed and everything is scripted to avoid mistakes in the demo. I was told by NSETS that this is a form of competition among schools; proving the NSETS are of value. I didn't have to endure this farce, but you will.

When you enter the school, you're expected to greet everyone in the teacher's room, including the principal and vice principal if they are on their way to their offices. To not do so would be a very grievous cultural faux pas, indeed. Greetings, for those of you not familiar with Far Eastern cultures, includes standing up (if you are sitting) and bowing. Just watch the Korean teachers, do as they do, and you'll be fine. These days, no matter whom I greet, I simply bob my head; I'm old enough to do so and get away with it.

In modern schools, the teacher's room will be heated. Way back in 1996, mine was heated with one portable kerosene heater situated in the middle of the room. You'll know when winter rolls around if you have heat or not, so be warned. I used to wear three layers of clothing in that room and felt pretty damn toasty for the most part. Korean winters can be rough on those coming from warm climates. Fortunately, I'm not one of them.

The classrooms, on the other hand, are rarely heated and, if they are, only certain classrooms will have heat. Many of the older schools use portable gas heaters – usually kerosene, which stinks to high heaven. Your clothing, your hair, your breath will reek of Kerosene. I would much rather tough it out in the cold than have to breathe in a kerosene-heated classroom. Fast forward to today, and you'll still find kerosene heaters; however, they've been much improved in terms of air pollution. You may also be teaching in more than one classroom, and some are warmer than others, depending on whether or not they're facing south. Newly constructed schools will almost always have heated classrooms.

Conversely, teaching during the summer months can be abysmally hot and humid if the classrooms have no air conditioning, and many do not. The humidity is unbearably high and no amount of fans can change that. Unfortunately, Korean schools are a conglomeration of concrete and brick, which spells doom for retention of heat in the winter, and breath in the summer. Again, these days most classrooms have AC, so things are getting better for teachers regarding comfort.

One of the downsides of the EPIK program for this teacher was all the preparation I had to do, which at the time really never bothered me much. I had to stay at the school from 8:30 to 4:30, and you will too, so you'll have quite a lot of time on your hands. During non-contact time, I prepped texts, photocopied game sheets, discussed and rehearsed lessons with my KETs, and researched what activities would be suitable for the classes I was teaching. All in all, I devoted from one to two hours per day on my lesson plans and sometimes much more.

Much of this will depend on your school and your KET. If you have a cooperative KET, you'll accomplish much, if not, well...grab the tequila. Nowadays, however, lesson planning isn't quite so intense, so you'll have a few hours desk warming to do.

Many of the public schools will demand that you submit lesson plans. This is usually handled by the KET, but I've heard of EPIK teachers also having to do their own; so be ready for that. The lesson plan format is different than that of the West, so I've include an example in the materials chapter for you to peruse. These days, I rarely spend more than 20 minutes prep work for my college classes, which is fine by me. I've paid my dues, sang the blues, now it's time for this teacher to reap the benefits of 17 years hard work. Adios to lesson plans.

If you're teaching middle school, you will have to teach all three grades. Furthermore, you may find that your duties include lesson planning and presentation of lessons as stated earlier. You may also have to write test questions, teach after-school classes, teach teacher's classes, and, if you were really born under a bad sign, plan and implement summer camps.

So long as the KET maintains discipline, things generally go quite well. Again, the name of the game, folks, is creativity; the more the better, at least in elementary school.

As the weeks go by, the students will become adjusted and relaxed with you in the classroom, so participation generally increases, and some, thank heavens, will actually look forward to your presence in class, which is largely dependent on which grade you find yourself teaching. And a word on games: if you limit games to once a week, you should be fine. When playing games, you'll come to know just how competitive Korean students can be. Again, you must be flexible in class and go with the flow, despite the game chaos.

Your KET may disagree with a lesson plan that includes games, but try to explain to him/her the purpose of the game. If it's educational, your KET may be more inclined to participate, but *don't* bet on it. If time allows, a game or two can be just what the doctor ordered. I've already discussed how Korean children have next to no childhood, so a game will give them the opportunity to have fun. Nothing wrong with that, folks. Beware, however, because they will have games on their minds all week.

Outside the classroom, particularly in middle and high school, students sometimes revert to hayseed antics: girls will laugh at you and may attempt to speak English, boys will generally do the same, and both will point at you and laugh to their cohorts. With younger Koreans, you'll find this behavior every now and then, regardless if the students are yours or not. As difficult as it may be, don't get upset over this. If students are sincere, and you'll know who they are by the way they express themselves, go ahead and speak with them. Many are not, however, and act like children much younger than their age belies.

These days, I haven't a lot of patience for these antics because most are not well-intended. I've learned to live with them, yes, because that's the way Korean children are, for better or worse. They may laugh at the foreigner, but, meanwhile, the foreigner learns to dislike Korean children.

Among many foreign teachers here, Korean children will go down in the annals of history as some of most disliked for reasons such as this. I've even heard many teachers complain about students swearing at them if they did not respond to the children's (usually middle and high school children) queries. Whether or not those students understand the meaning of swear words is debatable. Nevertheless, it is very disconcerting to hear them practice swearing, particularly when it is directed at you.

Again, when sincere, I have no problem with students trying out what they've learned in the English classroom. There are limits to my tolerance, however, and swearing is one of those. To be fair, this issue has improved within the last four to five years, thank god.

While on the subject, I recently had a high-school student approach me in a department store while I was at the checkout line. "*Are you a foreigner?*" He asked. My reply? "*What in hell?*" Yes, I know, not very nice, right?

Well, I was simply shocked at what a pointless question it was. Perhaps my brown hair, blue eyes and fair complexion had something to do with my reply? My point is this: if you don't like attention, negative or positive, you may want to try teaching elsewhere. With the exception of the larger cities in Korea, you're going to generate no small amount of interest. This is a small issue made large by endless repetition.

Nowadays, when I happen upon other foreign teachers on the streets, they carry with them what my sociology professor called *"studied avoidance"* that they have picked up as a result of certain Korean's behavior toward them. Most will not make eye contact, very few will greet you, and many walk hurriedly toward their destinations. Granted, many of them behave that way normally. Part of my point is that you probably don't want to become one of them. If you do, you are a victim.

Enough of that; let's get back to school. You will be expected to participate in *all* extra-curricular activities. These include Sports Day, wherein parents, teachers, and students compete in activities designed for each grade; field trips, which are quite obvious, and a few more. I remember looking forward to these activities because they afforded me a break from the monotony of the classroom/office routine. However, if you're not the type that likes being the center of attention, as mentioned previously, you're not going to like some of these activities much. Koreans teachers are the masters of pressure, (Tiger Teachers) thus, you may find yourself participating regardless of your distress at having to do so.

Be aware of *"emergency time,"* also, and this applies to everyone living in Korea. Emergency time is similar to a fire drill in the West. The outstanding difference, however, is that one prepares students for fire, the other for an invasion by North Korea, earthquakes, and sea-related disasters. The procedure is pretty easy; tune the TV to the national video, and when you hear the siren, escort the students out of the classroom to a predestinated meeting place. If you have a KET in the room, he/she will take care of everything.

There are also times when you have half-days and actually get to dress casually, such as midterms, finals, and speaking tests. Again, these half-days are a wonderful break in an otherwise monotonous schedule, even if they do confuse your lesson plans.

Teacher meetings, or so they're called here, are pretty casual affairs. They involve getting together at a restaurant and having dinner. These dinners can be a bit quiet and reserved at times, depending on who attends. Older teachers, particularly women, are not the party-goer types, so the younger teachers are always very respectful and reserved around them. But much of the time, the older teachers leave when dinner is finished, which livens up the crowd greatly. You can pretty much expect to be the focus of a lot of the conversation among the teachers, so get used to it and don't be rude. Just answer their questions as well as you can and all will go well.

After dinner, the more adventurous go to a bar or a norebong (karaoke room). I've had a lot of good times at both, but like the norebong in particular because I once was a musician, among other occupations. The norebong will give you a chance to know your Korean counterparts, and they, you. You'll be expected to drink alcohol, but not a lot. If for some reason you're a teetotaler, you can get off the hook by saying you have health or religious issues that won't allow you to drink alcohol. They will more than likely understand, unlike many folks I've known while teaching for corporations.

Ride that Clothes Horse!

Yes, I know, it's cliché; but when in Rome, do as the Trojans do. Okay, so I've livened it up a little; you get the idea.

Men, dress reasonably well. The public school venue is *not* the hagwon. Many folks here dress like every day is a fashion show, regardless if they're teachers or not. Break out the nice dress shirt, slacks, shoes, and a tie, which is what the Korean male teachers will be wearing 99.9 percent of the time. When it gets unbearably hot, however, I've seen many teachers lose the tie, so watch them and do as they do.

Women, ahem, my ex sometimes wore jeans but that was rare, indeed. When she did, there was usually some casual event going on at the school. At all other times, however, she dressed quite nicely. Again, simply watch what your Korean counterparts do and clone. Dressing nicely here gives the impression that you're professional and able to do the job. As an aside, I've never once worn a tie in 17 years of teaching in Korea, but that's me. I possess super powers that you don't, so don't try it.

Etiquette is yet another book for the future, so I really can't address it here at length. That doesn't mean it's not important; it's *incredibly* important to this culture. For the time being, I suggest doing an internet search and gathering the information there.

Areas of Discontent: I'm NOT a Happy Camper!

Negativity abounds regarding the EPIK program, and I feel it in your best interest to highlight some of this negativity, so you'll have no surprises going in should you decide to choose this venue.

In reality, EPIK has no centralization or standardization, so schools in each province vary, and, sometimes, vary greatly.

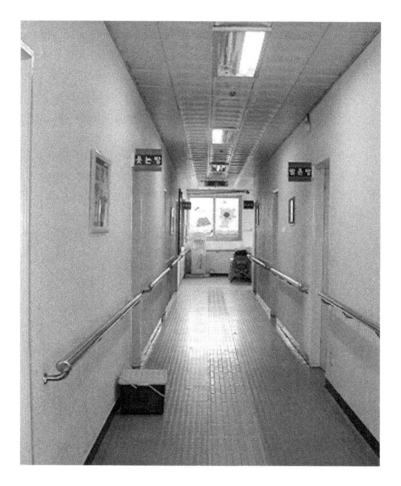

I've already discussed the fact that many contractual elements depend on the province and the schools within that province, so be ready for that. You may argue a contract point with your POE until the cows come home, but you'll only end up with a lot of manure.

And a word about the EPIK coordinator; back in the day, the coordinator of EPIK was absolutely of no value to us after leaving KNUE to begin teaching at our designated school. Fast forward to today, and many NSETS tell me that not much has changed. After you leave KNUE, you're left to fend for yourself with occasional input from your KETs or, rarely, your POE.

I hear so much negatively among EPIK NSETs that I'm a bit overwhelmed by it all. I really don't know what to make of it, but I will say this; if you're not a flexible person, you're going to have all kinds of grief trying to function in this system. There seems no end to complaints regarding KETs, student management, and feelings of worthlessness in the system.

What should you take away from this? Simply that maybe the government programs are not for you. Keep in mind that the more flexible you are, the more you'll be prepared for this venue should you decide that you can tolerate all of the nonsense. The Korean educational system is without a doubt one of the best examples of Murphy's Law, so if you understand that going forward, you'll be prepared for the worst.

What you do not want to do is become victim of EPIK's glowing propaganda during your orientation. Take any of the booklets and handouts that offer nothing but praise for the program and flush them. The same goes for the dinners where you must listen to glowing praise of the EPIK program from well-rehearsed lectures from KETS and NSETS. EPIK does not invite discontent during any of its orientation. However, you have this book, oh wise reader, so you can invite discontent by addressing these problems (good luck).

Again, KETs are the major complaint among NSETS, so I offer this: if Korea wishes to have NSETs in the classrooms, all KETs should be well-qualified to teach English just as all NSETs should be qualified. KETs that cannot communicate in English, cooperate with NSETs, be present in class at all times, help write lesson plans, and attend to classroom management should be retrained to do so. Yet another issue is how best to utilize NSETs, which, as stated, is a major concern among NSETs. EPIK really needs to define its goals, guidelines, and objectives so KETs and NSETs alike can use their contact time effectively

I also believe that KETs and NSETs should be able to evaluate one another's classroom performance, not just an evaluation of the NSET by the KET. These evaluations should be used to improve the effectiveness of both parties.

I discuss these issues with many NSETS, and they couldn't agree more. We all agree that disgruntled NSETs leave Korea in droves every year. Whether their reasons for leaving are valid or not, it still begs the question, what in the hell is happening? I was a teacher in this program, but I knew there would be all kinds of grief; the program was in its infancy, so ill winds did blow, and they blew hard. The program lost half of its teachers before their contract completion; so why a similar pattern 17 years later? It's certainly not the food, language, or cultural issues. What explanations are we left with then? I put this question to NSETs and found that they agree about one thing: the frustrations arising from being under-utilized to the point of absurdity.

I also hear a lot of negativity regarding not being a "real" teacher in the traditional sense. This seems insanely obvious, so why even remark on it? I've also been told that NSETs are nothing more than tape recorders and are in class for show only; that they are in class to provide *"edutainment"* and little more. Add to that, many in elementary and middle school feel that they are glorified babysitters. Their reasoning is that they teach only a fraction of the text and that grades are of no importance. To the above, I say you should be thankful to some degree. If you were a licensed teacher teaching solo in a Korean classroom setting, you would be as stressed, if not more so, than Korean teachers. Your work load would increase incrementally, so be thankful that you are what you are where you are. It could be so much worse, believe me.

Note, also, that it is not just NSETs that suffer from this chaotic system, but KETs and non-KET teachers alike. I personally know more than a few Korean elementary and junior high school teachers, and they continually complain of last minute schedule changes, disruptive students, bonehead parents, and so much more. Point is, don't feel singled out for suffering; it pretty much happens across the board.

And then there are the last minute schedule changes, and not knowing what is expected of you in advance. As Westerners, we really have a need to be kept in the loop, but this fact is lost on the EPIK people, your POE, and your KETs. It would surely seem that Korean education officials, as well as your principal, absolutely delight in keeping NSETs out of the loop. I find this unfortunate in that it would be so easy to plan in advance. As has been pointed out, however, KETs often don't know much in advance, either.

And while I'm at it, last minute class changes are not a big deal if you're ready for them. Always, and I mean *always* be ready for last minute schedule changes. Remember I mentioned Murphy's Law, right? Always have supplementary lessons or lesson plans on hand because you *will* experience schedule changes when you least expect them. Once schedule changes do occur, you'll be in a position to roll with them, leaving you relatively stress free. Ask yourself, then, can you tolerate all this dissension and dissatisfaction? If you can, you just might have a good year. If not, consider a hagwon position.

I must again stress that back in the day, the Koretta/EPIK program was one of the worst disasters to befall Korea in quite some time, so, even though the program is still very far from perfect, and never will be, it is not remotely close to the hell that it used to be.

Chapter 5

GePIK – Gyeongido English Program in Korea

L ike EPIK, Gepik places teachers in public schools to co-teach English. The program, again similar to EPIK, is not issue free. GePIK suffers the same dissatisfaction from last-minute scheduling changes, airfare, and settlement allowances that EPIK does. I can't recall the reference, but I read somewhere that of 950 teachers, 4.7 percent quit during the middle of the semester within the first year, and 34 percent quit during their first six months. These are not good numbers.

I did see a rather disturbing questionnaire being circulated around the net last year regarding the NSETS for GEPIK. Let's have a look at it.

"A questionnaire about the usefulness of the Native speaking English assistant teacher's classes" (For parents of students)

*Note that the grammar, usage, and spelling on the questionnaire are not mine. Questions asked on the survey included:

- Are you satisfied with the English language classes that utilize the native speaking teacher at the school your children currently attend? What is your reason?
- (Select all corresponding answers)
  1. Does not have teaching qualifications
  2. Not enough teaching ability
  3. Is not fluent enough in our language
  4. Does not have sufficient understanding of Korean culture
  5. Does not have sufficient understanding of the situation of Korean education
  6. Other comments
- Do you think that your children's comprehension/understanding is helped through the English classes that utilise the native speaking English teacher?
- In future, what do you think should be done regards the programme of using native speaking English teachers?
- Please write down the reasons why your children are dissatisfied or have struggled with their classes with the native speaking English teacher.
- If you have any opinions about the scheme of utilising native speaking English teachers please write them.

Have a look at number three, *"Not fluent enough in our language."* Is it just me, or am I mistaken when I ask are NSETS supposed to be teaching English, or learning Korean? This statement is an absurdity that borders on sheer lunacy. That and number four, "Does not have sufficient understanding of Korean culture." Most people with half a brain know that to teach language is to teach culture; it can't be avoided. NSETs are not teaching Korean, therefore Korean culture is of minor importance; cultural imperialism aside.

I present readers with this because it illustrates the lengths that the admins of these programs will go through to justify themselves and their job titles, not to mention please the Tiger Mothers. It doesn't bode well for the program, so you may want to use caution when considering this program, or you may find yourself on a plane home at your expense.

Furthermore, I've seen evidence that the program did not have the proper funding to pay its teachers. Translated into dollars and sense, it simply means that experienced teachers get the axe because their schools can no longer afford them. Those schools then hire a newbie because they are paid less than experienced teachers. *This is truly a program in trouble.*

Chapter 6

TaLK: Teach and Learn in Korea

The TaLK program is an after-school program organized by the Ministry of Education, Science and Technology. Last year, the ministry recruited a total of 380 native English speakers from five countries – the U.S., Canada, Australia, New Zealand, and the U.K. Most of those teachers consisted of ethnic Koreans from the countries that completed a month-long teacher-training program geared to sending them to underprivileged elementary schools across the country. Underprivileged is just a politically correct way of saying that you will usually be teaching at a rural school. But not always; my ex's school is in the center of the city and it has a TaLK teacher. Normally, however, the schools located in the country suffer from lack of exposure to native English teachers, thus the TaLK program. I believe that the program hoped to hire 650 TaLK teachers for 2013, thus giving the brave and adventurous undergrads a great opportunity to give it a go. What is unique about the program is that it hires undergrads, thus giving them a hell of an opportunity to get their teaching on, and discover whether or not Korea is for them. All TaLK teachers receive round-trip airfare, 1.5 million won per month, and a monthly accommodation allowance of 400,000 won.

Although the TaLK program does not pay as well as other venues, it's a bit more relaxed. I've never taught in this venue, obviously, but I know a few that currently do.

One of the TaLK teachers that I'm in touch with seems not to have any major complaints. He has told me, however, that the various levels of the students' English can be problematic, and that nearly half of his students were studying at hagwons. The hagwon students sometimes found the class boring and so caught up on their sleep. Those that didn't study at a hagwon found it a bit difficult to catch up; a classic case of language level disparity. Naturally, he wishes that he could pay more attention to those lagging behind, but he has 30 students in his classes, so they often get left behind and musty fend for themselves, just as they do in the public schools.

As in the hagwons, you should have a pretty damn good attitude toward children, because they are the target. Contact time is usually 15 hours per week. The rest of the time, you are pretty much left alone. The upside to this program is that you'll be placed in a rural setting. These rural schools are often really beautiful places, unlike their city counterparts that remind me so much of reformatory schools in the West. I would hazard to say that 95 percent of them are extremely well looked after. One sees manicured grounds, first or second growth trees, and flowers everywhere. It's all very picturesque, indeed. When I lived in an apartment (gulag) in the middle of the city, I used to take my sons to these schools on weekends so they could play in the playground, and I could simply breathe the country air.

But it's not only that. As said, these schools simply don't have the exposure to NSETS that the city schools do, so many of the students actually look *forward* to speaking English. By way of example, I have often walked into the C-store in the small village close to my country house, only to be accosted by middle school students wanting to practice what they've learned in real time, to the point of being a bit obnoxious. This doesn't often happen in the city.

And, while I'm praising the rural schools, I would be remiss if I failed to mention that the students simply have a better all-around attitude. I attribute this to their country upbringings. Many of them are still allowed a semblance of childhood and live in houses rather than high rise concrete gulags, (Correct: I dislike apartments) which really does have a huge impact on how they behave.

Keep in mind that some of these kids, and their Korean teachers, have never before met a foreigner up close and personal, so they're going to be watching you, believe me. I really hate the expression *"been there, done that,"* but I can't find a similar expression that does justice to my experience in the country setting. It used to be that NSETS were elevated to celebrity status. I even signed autographs back in the day. If you reside in a small community, you'll find that this celebrity status will still exist, albeit, to a lesser degree. You will, nevertheless, be given the title "*Our English Teacher*" by the villagers/townies.

TaLK teachers usually teach English conversation, writing, and practical English. Your job title is "*English Teacher for After-School Program.*" However, depending on the school and the students' needs, participants may also teach at a regular English class as an assistant.

If you desire to return to Korea after you graduate, a TaLK gig will look pretty good on a resume because, unlike a hagwon, it's a government sponsored gig.

Let me return to "*rural location*" for a moment. I'm from a rural community in the USA, so adjusting to rural life here has been a walk in the park for me. Just so, don't believe what the Korean talking points tell you about the countryside: safe? Yes. Clean? Well... Serene? Semantics. I've been awakened at 6:00am by a nut job with a portable mosquito fogger literally gassing me as I lay in bed. Well, it was summer, so all of my windows and doors were open.

Worse yet, many small Korean communities are hard wired into a community PA system. Huge loud speakers are strategically placed on power line poles around the villages. The original intention was in case of emergencies, such as North Korea having another go at South Korea. I've got one of these babies about a stone's throw from my front door. You want misery? How about another nut job announcing a road closure at 5:00am Sunday morning over the PA at 130db? This after an all-nighter of dancing with the Tiger until 3:00am. Semantics, folks, semantics.

TaLKies will sometimes teach with a Korean teacher, which, depending on the KET, can make things easier in most cases, particularly with classroom management issues, which are not nearly as serious as they are in the city schools. As in other public school venues, you'll be expected to participate in all school activities. And, similarly, you'll probably be asked to use a prescribed text. However, the TaLKie in my village has been given the gift of preparing his own lessons.

Many have complained how the TaLK administration, much like EPIK's, will have nothing to do with you after you've settled at a school. That said, don't expect support from them if you encounter difficulties. You may also, as per usual, have communication difficulties with KETs and school officials. Don't sweat this too much; try to negotiate meaning as best you can via your Korean/English electronic dictionary. If you don't have one, get one.

You will also have to have an apostilled degree and a criminal background check completed if you are no longer an undergrad, so if you're interested in this venue, plan on obtaining these documents at least 3 months in advance. These 2 requirements, sadly, are becoming standard for nearly any teaching position in Korea.

If you dress semi-casual, you'll be OK. This is, really, a semi-casual teaching venue. Your students, however, may take your instruction pretty damn seriously, though.

Qualifications: Can I do it?

I'll simply outline candidate qualifications because you will find all of the pertinent information on the TaLK website. So let's begin:

- You must have either obtained an Associate's degree or be enrolled in a Bachelor's program and completed at least 2 years of study. Ethnic Koreans who are in their 1st or 2nd year of college/university are eligible also, as are university graduates and graduate school students

- Be able to communicate in English fluently with clear and distinct pronunciation.
- Meet the criteria of eligibility for E-2 (F, foreign Language Instructor), F-4 (Overseas Koreans), or F-2 (Spouse of Korean national) visa set forth by the Korean Immigration Authority

Preference is given to the following candidates:

- Have or will have a degree in education, English or subjects related to Korea.
- Have excellent school records including good command of English
- Have completed primary and secondary education in the countries aforementioned.

Here's one major caveat for ethnic Koreans, one that I will also have to consider as my sons become of age:

- ***Any male with Korean citizenship who has not fulfilled his military duty or received an official waiver must choose the six-month contract term***
- If you are an overseas Korean with less than two years of university education as of February 2010, you MUST apply for an F-4 Visa. Therefore, inquire at the Korean Embassy/Consulate General whether you meet the F-4 visa qualifications before you apply. * If you are a foreigner without Korean heritage, you MUST have completed two or more years of education at a university or graduated from a college as of February 2010 to be eligible for the program
- After arriving in Korea, you must undergo a medical check-up at a designated hospital, and if the test results determine that you have any serious disease(s) which are infectious or may keep you from performing your duties (e.g. drug addiction or AIDS),

your assignment is canceled and you must return to your home country

Contract term:

- The contract terms are for the duration of either 6 months or one year. The contract may be extended for an additional period not to exceed 2 years in total.
- The POE will decide placements. Participants will work at elementary schools within the POE. Rejection of placement may result in disqualification from the program.
- List of placements: Incheon, Gangwon, Chungbuk, Chungnam, Gyeongbuk, Gyeongnam, Daegu, Ulsan, Busan, Jeonnam, Jeju, Jeonbuk, *(Author's note: these are provinces in Korea. And, yes, I live in Jeonbuk. Bravo! Also note that Seoul, Gyeonggi Province, and Gwangju do not participate in the TaLK program.)*

Accommodation

- The POE (Provincial Office of Education) will decide the type of accommodation for each NSET.
- If an NSET does not wish the POE to provide accommodation, a rent subsidy (a fixed fee of 400,000 KRW) will be provided instead.

* Any and all fees, charges, costs, taxes, expenses, etc. incurred in using the apartment, shall be borne by the individual.

Round-trip airfare

- A one-way economy class airfare of the most direct one-way flight available from the international airport nearest your place of residence to Incheon Airport and a return air ticket at the completion of your contract term entitlement.

If your scholarship is canceled during the contract term, a return air ticket will not be provided.

Other benefits

- Preparatory Orientation is held for four weeks upon arrival to Korea and before being placed in schools. Examples of workshops to attend: teaching & learning methodology, understanding Korean lifestyle and culture, theories and practices for classroom management.

Vacation Leave

- Six-month contract : 7 business days
- One year contract : 14 business days (7 business days per semester)

Chapter 7

Kindergartens

A h...the **K** word. If you dote on children, this one is for you. If you don't, well...you know the drill. The problem is that more than a few hagwons have at least one kindergarten class, so you may end up teaching these youngsters regardless if you like it or not. Not only that, some hagwons have more than one Kinder class, so be warned. Each class will likely have different age groups - beginning at three and ending at eight years of age.

Nearly all private kindergartens have English classes. Last year, an official from the Korean Ministry of Education conducted a survey of 274 private kindergartens across the country and found that 262, or 96 percent, provide English classes. The kindergartens were found to have invested an average of 2.7 million won (2,520 USD) for English education facilities. Also, 44 percent of them had native English speakers. Incidentally, this same official further stated there were many unqualified English-speaking teachers at the kindergartens. Asked why they provide English classes, 66 percent stated demands from parents, 13.4 percent stated competition with other kindergartens, and 10.3 percent said the government's policy toward strengthening English education.

Any way you look at it, dear readers, more and more English education institutes for preschoolers have appeared, burdening parents with yet more financial stress. Welcome again to English education in Korea.

On a personal note, I've had many professionals in Korea ask me if I would teach their preschoolers, to which *I would answer: I only babysit my own children these days.*

As difficult as it may be to imagine, even to me, I've co-taught kindergarteners at a private kindergarten. I was there mostly to model the language; an English mouth piece, if you will. There were two other adults present: a

KET, and a classroom teacher for classroom management, which, if you know the kiddies, can be a hair-pulling experience. Such cute little people, tabula rasa – blank slate - ready to learn whatever is taught. I've got to admit, I enjoyed the little people. It was actually a blessing in disguise; I would soon have children of my own, so I knew what to expect once I did.

Contact time was limited to 20 minutes, which was more than enough given children's short attention spans. I taught three classes in the morning, ate lunch at the school and finished up with three classes after lunch. We focused on phonics, listening, singing, dancing, all in the target language. They had a blast, and so did I for the most part.

Those of you who find yourselves in this venue will want to keep instruction limited and basic. You absolutely must make language learning fun, to do otherwise just won't cut it. You'll lose them to hundreds of distractions around them. And, ladies, watch out for breast grabbing. And urine. And saliva. Whether male or female, you'll quickly find a teaching apron your best friend.

That was a good gig. However, you may not be so lucky, and find yourselves teaching longer than 20 minutes with no KET. That's OK as long as you have a homeroom teacher present. If not, you *are* going to suffer, no way around it. That's why patience is a virtue. You'll be continuously tested. If you do have to teach longer than 20 minutes, pace yourself, or you'll not make it through the day because you want to include dancing and singing and many other kinesthetic activities in your syllabus that will tire you.

Chapter 8

Universities

L et's begin with this: beginning in 2008, the Korean government invested $804 million USD over five years to attract foreign professors. How nice is that? Even old timers call this the most envied position in Korea. Well to them, I say *no way*. Try privates. Glorious, blissful... Just so, universities are indeed a good gig. Let's see why:

1. Civilized contact hours: unlike hagwons or the EPIK program, many universities ask from 9 to 22 contact hours per week. How great is that? Pretty damn great, I'm here to say.

2. Office hours: most ask for one office hour per day, after which you're free to do as you wish.

3. Private office: at worst, you'll have to share with one other teacher.

4. Better quality students: caveat – it depends on the school.

5. Freedom to create your own curricula: just do it.

6. Vacation: I love this one. My first job gave us nearly 5 months paid vacation per year. Caveat: you may be asked to teach special classes (English camps) during the vacation.

7. Computer + internet: bored? Surf away!

8. Higher wages: university jobs usually begin at 2K per month, with wage increases for recontracting. However, in the last 7 years, this wage has NOT increased.

9. University women: hold the phone! How did that get in here?

A Great Gig

1. Contact hours: Yes, that's right: 9 to 22 hours per week. In reality, however, I would hazard that most require at least 14 per week. It all depends on student enrollment. If enrollment is up, expect more contact hours, if enrollment is down, expect less. Therefore, I always hoped that enrollment was down, naturally. What is great here is that no matter how little you teach, you'll be paid the same, regardless.

Back in the nineties, though, things weren't quite so easy with the rural universities. I remember teaching 24 contact hours per week and having to teach eight hours back to back more than once. Again, that was my introduction to teaching at a university. When I began speaking to other university teachers, I discovered that they typically taught no more than 20 hours per week and never had more than a four hour block.

Typically, classes are two hours each, two to three times per week. However, there are schools that have one hour classes, actually 50 minutes. If you do have to teach two hour classes, you'll be given a break 10 minutes before the first hour is up and will be able to end class five minutes early, which works out to an hour and forty minutes per class. I'll tell you how to teach two hour classes later.

Related to the above is class size, which can run from 10 to 60 students per class, again depending on enrollment.

I once had a class with 72 students and many classes with over 50 students. I would not wish that on anyone. Just this year, however, the ministry of education began evaluating universities. Those schools that overpopulated (most) their classrooms were given poor evaluations. Therefore, many schools began hiring professors in any discipline that was overpopulated. Naturally, English professors were included.

2. Office hours: Office hours are a breeze with one exception: final grades. This week can be pure, unadulterated hell on teachers, no matter if you're foreign or native. You *will* have students upset over their grades, and many of them will ask that you change their grades to something more acceptable. I've even had students show up at my office with their mothers! The big, and I mean *big*, problem with some universities is that they demand you grade on a curve, which is pure nonsense. We can thank the Korean professors for that cupcake: many of them inflated scores whether or not their students were deserving of them. With the curve, many students who deserve good grades end up getting a lesser grade. Other than that, office hours are lonely. I usually had a few drop-ins a few times per week wanting to practice English with a native speaker, so no sweat there.

3. Private office: Yes, readers, a place of your own, particularly if you've just come from EPIK where you're one of 10 to 30 other teachers in the teacher's room. Some of the better universities will even repaint your office to your color choice. At a minimum, you'll have a desk, office chair, computer, and a file cabinet. Options include a couch, student chairs, a sink, air conditioner, and bookshelves. These offices are not, for the most part, heated. Most of the Korean professors have large units in their offices that provide air conditioning in the summer and heat in the winter, or they simply use portable electric heaters. Your

office, in all likelihood, will not have these units unless you are fortunate enough to teach at a newly built school or a higher quality school.

The offices themselves can be spartan to impressive. I've had both. Most have more than enough square feet, so you can stretch out quite nicely, if you wish. I have, in the past, had to share an office space with one other teacher on three occasions. Two of those times turned out to be hell. As an aside, the university officials know that you are just passing through, as it were. They will not go out of their way, in most cases, to accommodate your office. However, you will be free to do so yourself. At my first university, I never bothered. They moved me around so much that I soon gave up trying to make an office homey. However, later schools proved more stable, so I began to clone my Korean colleagues. Many of their offices look more like living rooms than offices.

Better Quality of Students

I actually dreaded having to deal with this subject, and almost deleted it entirely from the book. You see, oh kind and loyal reader, this is yet another book in and of itself, so the challenge here is to condense this information into a compact version of a book. I accept the challenge, but I'm not happy about it.

I'll attempt to background universities, so you'll better understand the nature of Korean universities and students.

There exists in Korea a proliferation of universities. The province in which I teach has, at last count, 15 four-year universities; eight more than the large and wonderful state that I'm from in the USA. The better ones are, for the most part, government owned. They are the National universities. The others, privately owned, are located in the countryside. I've seen many private universities that sit out in the boondocks with nothing around them but rice paddies and small villages. I taught at one such university, but more on that later.

There are exceptions to the quality and location of private universities. There are in Seoul and its satellite cities many private universities that rank in the top five in Korea. Elsewhere, however, they run the gamut from good to absurd. Naturally, the national universities are less expensive than the privates. Most private universities are, by Korean standards, very expensive. However, even these offer funding options: scholarships, loans, etc.

While in high school, students who are interested in attending a university must take the dreaded CSAT. Most students take these exams very seriously, and put their noses to the grindstone. However, there are just as many that don't. The short version: if they do well, they may be accepted to one of the better universities, of which 90 percent reside in and around Seoul. If they do poorly, on the other hand, they may end up at a private university somewhere in god-knows-where Korea.

Just so, not every student, or, more to the point, every parent, can afford one of the universities in Seoul or its satellite cities. They are the elite schools in Korea, and their tuition, housing, etc., reflect this elite status. Thus, they must settle for a more reasonably priced education; but not always. My ex's cousins sold everything they owned lock, stock, and barrel to send their son to med school in Seoul. Fortunately for them, he graduated, opened a clinic in Busan, and has compensated his parents quite well, thank you.

But this is not always the case. Many parents do the same, but with no return on their investment. Their child fails and, therefore, the parents fail, too. The parents wind up in a barely habitable, small, old, nasty apartment or container (yes, a converted shipping container.) They are old, alone, and abandoned by the very children they sacrificed everything they had for. Worse yet, they are at an age when they should be able to relax and enjoy what remaining life they have. They are truly miserable.

Allow me to say this: The better schools do seem to have better quality students. What qualities? To begin, they generally take their studies seriously. English, unless it's a major, is not really taken seriously by most rural university students. And why should it? If students don't have a reasonably good command of the English language by the time they enter university, what good will three to six hours per week do them? This is the attitude among most students in private schools who did not do well on their entrance exams. Furthermore, many are aware that their futures are limited to jobs that will not require a great command of English. They are, for the most part, simply content to get a passing grade.

However, students in the national universities and the better private schools do indeed take English seriously. And not just because it gets a grade just as all other subjects do thus affecting their GPA. They have grand ambitions and know damn good and well that the folks who do the hiring will take a very serious look at their grades, so they're really motivated to do well. They are also aware that many job interviewers will test their English skills. Many students are further motivated because they use the lower quality schools as stepping stone to one of the better schools. I have lost many wonderful students during their third year of study because they transferred to better schools.

Let's have a look at the quality of students in the rural schools. To frame this, know that I've had some really good times with my students in and out of class. Most were sincere and would always show at least a modicum of respect. However, finding students who had a desire to excel at English was rare, indeed. Most of the provincial private universities are glorified adult day care centers that cater to those who wish to party and catch up on their lost childhood. If you, too, are a party animal and don't take teaching seriously, welcome home.

I do, however, understand the party culture. As mentioned, graduation from the hell known as high school is a monumental event, and freedom from the many obligations of their past lives is worthy of celebration. And then there is the need to find who they are, experience a social life, and develop their interests. In contrast, Western students have more than enough - perhaps too much - time to develop themselves through such activities as sports, school clubs, dances, and building relationships with other students while in high school. Korea, as you have seen, offers very little of the above. Middle and high school students, tragically, have little time to explore life outside the textbook, hagwon, and micro-management of their Tiger Mothers. Finally, at least for the males, they fully realize that mandatory military service is looming ahead after their sophomore year. This is not a pleasant thought for most of them. Naturally, they are aware that they had better party hard while they have time because once in the military, they quickly come to understand that it's time to get damned serious. As an aside, I've had many students leave school for the military, only to return completely changed in almost every way. What was once an immature student has returned a very responsible and mature adult.

As absurd as it may sound, I could always predict how the students would do within the first two weeks of teaching. You know the drill, and perhaps you were one of them: students who wished to participate sat in front of the class, while those who had little or no desire, confidence, or were too nervous, sat in the back. Those in the middle, well, they were undecided, as it were. So, based on that seating order, I would make grade predictions, and 90 percent of the time those predictions were correct. And, no, it was not a self-fulfilling prophecy.

You see, Korean students, depending on the school, are a whole different crowd. Their behavior, in and out of class, seems childish and naive compared to the West. Indeed, the girls will go to ridiculous lengths to retain their youthful behavior and appearance, which I understand given Korean culture. But an 18 to 24 year old acting like a 16 year old high school girl really becomes annoying. In the private universities, I dreaded seeing trophy women in class and having to listen to the whiny cut-your-wrist intonation they use when addressing the males—*opah!* (big brother). Certain exceptions did exist; the women in childhood education classes were very sincere and mature. Simply put, many of the others were there to find husbands and in saying so, I believe I'm being too kind.

The guys aren't quite so unpleasant. However, every class had a few smart-asses, who thought they were somehow more special than the rest. I can remember having to deal with these characters on many occasions. These students can be stressful to teachers and very disruptive to students who are sincere, so it's best to deal with them as soon as possible. Remember folks, you're a teacher, not a babysitter.

I'm proud to say that, in the seven years that I've taught at universities, I've walked out on one class, only. It was a nightmare; like something you see in the inner city high schools in the U.S where chaos reigns supreme. My God, no matter what I did, I couldn't get anyone's attention or get them to behave, so in desperation, I yelled at the top of my lungs and told them I would fail them all, gathered my books and walked out.

Well, I knew I couldn't fail them all, as much as I would have liked to. So, during the next class with them, I gave them a handout written in Korean stating that if they did not wish to attend class, they did not have to. This was in conflict with university policy, but there was no way that I was going to spend three months with those students. Long story short, the handout did the job. After taking attendance, one third of them walked out, leaving me with about six students. Perfect! I'm no angel, folks. As the saying goes, I don't angry, I get even. And I did when final grades rolled around. When you fail a student, that student must take the class again, so they would be one of the other foreign teacher's problems. This was before the university implemented the grade curve policy, so I had no difficulties failing 12 students, as shocking as that might sound. When you're in a situation such as this, you quickly learn how to play the game in the trenches. You try to retain a bit of professionalism, but sometimes shit just happens.

Again, you'll find that students who have completed their mandatory military service to be among your best, and sometimes, only, serious students. Not once was I given grief by a veteran student; and, many years later, I'm proud to call several of them my friends.

And then there are the students who show up for class during midterm and final tests, only. These students fully expect to be passed. Heads up on this one, readers, there exists in some Korean universities, good and bad, pressure to pass as many students as possible. This pressure is sometimes explicit and sometimes implicit. For example, I remember teaching a night class for business administration students. None of these students were below 38 years of age. They were all employed and their employers demanded a university degree of them, so, there they were.

Because of their age, they were great students, I must say. But also due to their age, I could do little to help them. Most of their language problems had fossilized beyond what I could do in one semester, so I did what I could to get them through as painlessly as possible. Several of them, however, just couldn't get with the program, and they knew it. One night before class, the dean of business administration wished to speak with me about those students. So, there the four of us were, all seated in the dean's office. The dean was a real gentleman - soft spoken, kind, and an all-around great guy who, after many years, is still a friend. Koreans professors, such as the dean, rarely get straight to the point, unlike their Western counterparts. No, they will ask how you are, make you feel welcomed and comfortable with small talk, offer a drink, and just generally put you at ease before getting to the heart of the matter. When they do get to the point, you may have trouble recognizing it, it comes so tacitly.

He explained why these older students found themselves in my class. I assured him that I did indeed understand, and that I would do everything, within reason, to help them. The dean knew of my reputation for having little tolerance for student nonsense, and my record of failing students, so he was a little nervous about the two problem students in my class. In sum, if you haven't learned the art of compromise, Korea will teach you. Incidentally, when I had lunch with him last week, this same professor told me that the quality of the students attending the university was not getting better since I left; it was getting worse.

And then there are the students who do not show up at all. Yes, you read that right. They, too, expect to be passed. Maybe they were working overseas and couldn't attend class. Just so, I would never pass them, despite angry phone calls, denunciations of my character, and negative reports to the department chair. If I had to do it all over again, I still wouldn't pass them. I'm still amazed that these things happen at an institution of higher learning.

Let's get to the cream of crop: the National universities scattered about, and the private universities in and around Seoul and a few places in the other provinces. Students in these schools, for the most part, are great to teach. None of the awful trench warfare that happens in the rural schools will happen in the top schools. Best of all, you'll even be challenged by the students in class, which almost never happens in the rural schools. Seasoned teachers know how great it is when students challenge us; it makes us teach on our feet, do our homework, and be prepared for those challenges. In sum, we become better teachers. At the lower quality schools, one tends to become incredibly lazy and uninspired, which does not make for a good teacher.

Student behavior is the antithesis of the rural schools. Students are fun, reasonably bright, if not naive; and almost never sleep in class due to a night of heavy drinking. The Korean professors are also sharper. I've noticed that within the two private rural schools that I had taught at, the professors in the Department of English, with but one exception, have not moved within the last 17 years. No upward mobility for them; they just don't have the right stuff. However, at the better schools, I've had to say regretful goodbyes to more than one professor who moved up the professorial ladder to an even better school.

At one school, I came to know a few English professors who were known internationally. They were well published and respected by their cohorts in Korea and abroad. They were fluent in English and able to write very comprehensive research essays, etc. You'll rarely find this at the rural schools. Oh, yes, a professor might publish a paper or two, but they rarely leave Korea. Add to that, you never know how or why the professor got hired. In Korea, it is, or was, possible to make huge financial donations to a university. Once this was done, the job candidate had a very good chance of being employed as a professor.

Most of the good schools will have you use texts that they or the foreign liaison/staff have chosen. Again, this can be a real pain in the butt. I've never had a good school choose an honest to god worthwhile text – they don't exist. If you are fortunate to choose your own texts, count your blessings; you'll have a much better time. If not, deal with it. I repeat; if you've been given a lemon, grab the tequila. While teaching for my first rural university, I was free to choose my text. I used this experience to find a reasonably awful one but would change texts every semester, nevertheless. Long story short, I never did find one that I liked.

You'll find that the top schools have a variety of English programs: business English, writing, conversation, creative, tourism. In some schools, you'll have a choice as to which programs you wish to teach during each semester. Other schools will not give you a choice; you'll have to teach what they demand of you.

Contact hours are generally the same, or a bit less in some schools. You'll have anywhere from 9 to 22 contact hours per week. However, many of these schools will have extra work for you if you so choose. This extra work runs the gamut from just about everything imaginable. I used to be pretty enthusiastic about extra work because it paid so damn well. These days, no way; my sons are my extra work.

As stated earlier in the book, the only real issue with the better schools is the damned grade curve. During final grade week, my office was always full, as well as my email accounts. Many students weren't happy, and deservedly so; they did indeed earn higher scores but the curve wouldn't allow for it. How to deal with it? Change their grades. The school officials may not like it, but to hell with them. If a student earned an A, I would always deal with the officials and have the grade changed. However, not every school uses a curve, there are just as many that use exact grading.

Other than that, smooth sailing, folks. These students have a bit of class; something lacking at the rural schools. Oh, yes, the students are kind, but they simply don't have the motivation. They are, debatably, very lazy when it comes to English, whether or not you're a good teacher. I attribute this to the fact that they simply are not interested in English as a means of communication; rather, they attend class hoping that it might in some way help them achieve a higher TOEIC/OPIc score. Not only that, English is mandatory at many schools. Forcing a language upon an unwilling crowd seems a bit pointless. English should be an elective, at least in Korea.

As an aside, but much related to the subject, is that 100 percent of Korean parents wish their children to attend university. You have already read about the stress this creates among middle and high school students to the point of contemplating suicide. During 2009, an astounding 202 students actually did. The suicide rate in Korea is undoubtedly high: 15 per 100,000 25 to 24 year-olds. Compare that with ten Americans, seven Chinese, five Britons, and it's crystal clear that the system needs an overhaul. Thankfully, the suicide rate, beginning in 2009, has fallen, so things are looking up (pun intended).

Yet another storm on the horizon is one similar to that of the USA: because so many students attend university, competition for what few jobs exist, particularly white collar is incredibly intense. In fact, Korean students with vocational training, while not getting a white collar position, do indeed find it much easier to find employment than those who pursue an academic degree. One survey, I can't remember the source, stated that 40 percent of university graduates still had not found jobs four months after graduation. And, so, parent's investment in their children's education does not always guarantee a worthwhile ROI.

I noticed changes to the system and hiring practices after the Korean financial crisis in 1997. The corporations began laying off thousands of workers in an attempt to stay afloat. After the crisis subsided, the corporations began hiring again only to find that there were hundreds of applicants for a simple entry-level position. This really put pressure on high school graduates to pursue an academic degree.

Further compounding the issue is the major corporations (chaebol) employ a very small percentage of the overall Korean workforce at ten percent. With that in mind, you'll come to realize what drives many Korean university students at the top 10 universities.

Looking back, I should have been more flexible regarding the party culture at the lower quality schools. I had only been in Korea for one year when I began teaching at university, so I simply wasn't informed. Fortunately for you, oh trusted reader, you are and will continue to be informed.

Chapter 9

Miscellaneous Venues

Corporations

Corporations, it should be said, are for those of us who have been in the system for a while. In fact, many job postings for corporate teaching jobs state that you must be in-country and have had previous experience in the corporate world. Too, there are corporations that require a business degree. I've found this to be somewhat true. If you're not familiar with Korean norms and customs, you'll probably not want to apply to this venue until you've gained some knowledge and experience under your belt. Not knowing Korean corporate culture can be stressful, and give you no end of grief.

Most Korean corporations that hire are huge conglomerates. The Koreans call them *chaebol*. A few examples of chaebol are: Samsung, Hyundai, Lotte, Kia, Daewoo, and LG. Most chaebol have more than one division: shipbuilding, steel, automobiles, electronics. Because the chaebols do business overseas, each company professional must have a good command of English; thus, the English teachers.

When you work for a corporation, you are expected to be on the job site at least 8 hours. In that respect, you'll see very little difference between you and your Korean colleagues. Contact time varies; anywhere from four to six hours a day. You'll have some nice perks though, that make the long hours worthwhile:

- Nice office: non-shared with computer/internet.
- Small Classes: I don't think I've ever seen a class with over 12 students, and many times less. I have also seen corporations where you work one on one with students an hour a day, five days a week.
- No children.
- Nice lodging: Lodging varies from campus dorm style rooms on the job site to 14 pyoung (32 sq. ft.) apartments close to the job site. Again, exceptions do occur. I know of one ship building corporation where teachers had a pretty long commute to the job site from their lodging.
- Above average salary.
- Professional teaching environment: classrooms are fully equipped and air conditioned.

These days, corporations tend to outsource hiring to in-country recruiters. These recruiters handle everything: interviews, resumes, contracts, texts, and payment. They advertise the job, you apply, and, if accepted, teach at a location specified by the headhunter. I guess this saves the corporation money because they don't have to do full-time hiring.

With that in mind, it's rare indeed to find work as an in-house teacher for a corporation. I see maybe one or two positions per year. As said, this is due to outsourcing.

Most of us who have worked the corporate venue agree that overall, it's not a bad gig. Better than the hagwon, public/private schools, but not as good as the universities/colleges. The only drawbacks for this teacher were the long hours and prep time. Yes, a lot of prep time. If you're serious about your work, you'll want to really dig in and give your students the best that you can give, which means a lot of lesson planning. It's not at all like the hagwon where most inexperienced teachers can wing it. There are corporate students that come to you at all levels of English, so many know what's up, and, unlike many other venues, they will ask questions; the kind of questions that teachers live in fear of. So, you've got to be well prepared and be able to teach on your feet.

Generally, the teaching material is international business/presentation English with a small amount of social English thrown in. Unlike most general conversation texts, there are some pretty decent business texts. You will find that, at times, you'll not have a choice of textbook. You'll be given the one that the recruiter wants you to use. Naturally, you don't have to teach the text all the time. For example, I've used flash cards to create a game based on vocabulary building that the learners simply loved.

Not long ago, I contacted a recruiter based in Seoul about a job teaching business English to 15 company employees an hour's drive from my house. Because I could not interview in person, the recruiter stated that I must submit a video of my teaching, so she could gauge my expertise as well as my appearance and voice. Well, I didn't take too kindly to that suggestion; if my resume wasn't enough than to hell with her and to hell with her company.

This simply illustrates the importance that certain Koreans attach to appearance. God forbid that my skin color is something other than fair, or I used an English dialect unbecoming to the recruiter.

Obviously, I could regale you with many stories about teaching in this venue. However, I realize that none of them would be relevant to you because corporate teaching is for those of us with years of experience coupled with the right immigration status. Moreover, most of those stories involved alcohol, so I'll save them for another book on Korea.

Two Year Trade/Tech Schools

I won't dwell long on this venue because these schools rarely hire English teachers. However, a hagwon just might farm you out for one reason or another, so I'll simply do an outline. I have taught at one such school as a freelancer. This was a handshake contract. I agreed to their terms, they agreed to mine, we shook hands, and so it began.

Obviously, I did not teach English majors; they don't exist at tech schools. No, I was there because two students from each major had been promised a free semester in Australia or New Zealand by the school administration. That was the primary and, for most, only motivation. However, roughly half of the students were there to learn English, albeit very tentatively, to increase TOEIC scores

The students, however, were well-behaved. They might have a conversation while I taught, but I had no trouble cutting it short. Only once did a student come to class inebriated. After I finished with him, he never did it again. As an aside, this was the first time I had taught grandmothers. I can honestly say that I have now taught every age group and just about every background. I used to have some pretty rough times with those two grandmothers; they always wanted to speak Korean in class, so I found myself disciplining them. Naturally, they didn't like that given their ages. I would never advocate an *"English Only"* class, but those two were just too disruptive.

Language problems were abundant, as you may well have guessed. I experienced every kind of problem that I had encountered in the past plus a few more that the grandmas taught me.

Because of my teaching style, students soon discovered that my class would not be the walk in the park they may have thought, which accounted for a drastic drop in class numbers, I imagine. When teaching adults and adolescents, I really focus on suprasegmentals (prosody), which they were not taught by their Korean teachers. They had a difficult time, but I was setting them up to learn English independent of me. The brighter students understood, but the others found it a burden. Yet, according to many, I was their favorite teacher on campus. I taught them as individuals, and recognized them as such. Remember readers, it's not mistakes or errors that you are correcting, it's people. We were on a first name basis with each other, and we did have some very memorable times in class. Many wished they could continue to study with me, but tech schools are two year schools; thus, they said their sad goodbyes and began a job search or transferred to a four year school.

My ex-wife advised me to lighten up on these students and not take teaching so seriously, perhaps thinking that I wouldn't lose so many of them. They are not positively motivated, and they want 100 percent enjoyment, she explained. That's the way it is in the trade schools and provincial universities. I can never take such advice to heart. I love teaching, and I'm a dynamic teacher with the knowledge and experience to deliver the goods as well as anyone in Korea or elsewhere. To do otherwise would be nearly impossible. I show my enthusiasm in class via my methodology and wit, and I believe it's obvious to the brighter students that I'm really trying to help them.

As a part-timer, you will have no office of your own. You'll have a small room which you will share with other part-time and visiting teachers. That's not a problem, unless you want to use the computer; there are usually only a few in the room, so you'll have to wait your turn.

The pay was good. I taught two hours a day, five days a week, which earned me $2K. Not bad for 40 hours of work per month, I must say. But, in all honesty, I earned every penny of it. I was always exhausted after those two hours.

As stated, classes were 50 minutes each. I would spend at least 40 of those minutes pushing conversation, since that, and listening skills, was their weak point. You've always got to clue in to student goals and do proper assessments, so you can make the most effective use of your contact time. Most of those students, I knew, were going to spend time overseas where English was the L1, so I geared my syllabus accordingly. I also did my best to teach them the dialects used by the speakers in those countries which can be quite outstanding.

I used one text, only. Money is *always* a problem for Korean college students, so you will not want to stress their, or, in most cases, their parents' bank account too much. The text, which shall go unnamed here, was of my choice and was one of the best of the worst that I've found for recycling lessons, which is what you want in a good text should one ever exist.

Again, English is not taken seriously by most of these students. Related to that, the president of the college wanted me to teach him two times per week. He lasted a week, which speaks volumes. He could communicate at a high-intermediate level, but his English was difficult to comprehend due to many pronunciation issues. When I have to devote my entire self to listening/deciphering a person's English, I become a language doctor. He didn't like the fact that I was correcting him, due to his position, and felt humiliated and lost face. One week later, no more English. That, in a nutshell, is Korea.

Phone/Internet English

Well, let's see...how about phone or internet English? Yes, they're real. Teacher and student are paired up and use web cams to do the instruction/learning. There are a few options for learners - guided conversation for 10 to 50 minutes a day from Monday through Friday, or Monday, Wednesday, and Friday, using material prepared by the teacher or company.

This is a cheap alternative to the hagwon. It pays poorly, but if you have 13 or 14 students per day, you'll do okay.

I've noticed that English speakers from the Philippines more often than not take these positions.

English Villages

English villages are a relatively new venue to teaching English. They seemed to have been created to allow students to use what they have learned in a variety of contexts that hope to recreate what they may encounter in the West. Some villages have up to 53 experience classes, each with encounters in hospitals, subways, bus stations, airport immigration, and many more. These experiences take place in experience specific classrooms wherein students become actors in various roles such as physicians, restaurant waiters, police officers, store clerks. Naturally, they are taught the necessary vocabulary before performing these tasks.

Basically, what the villages do is bring the West to the East. Great concept in that it allows some overzealous parents an alternative to sending their children overseas, which separates the family and wastes thousands of dollars. However, the villages are *not* cheap, either.

Because these schools immerse students in English, you may be expected to teach 30 hours or more. It's not at all unusual to teach nine hours a day Monday through Saturday. Yes, you read that right – Saturday.

Most villages have regular, intensive English programs as well as winter and summer camps. You'll be expected to teach at them all. As an English village teacher, be prepared for preschoolers, because there is a good chance that you'll have them in one of your classes.

I've had some village teachers tell me that they enjoyed the village experience more than a hagwon gig. A few stated that variety was key to that enjoyment. Be aware that you'll be expected to act, sing, dance, and role-play. If you're uncomfortable with these, you may want to look at other venues. Villages tend to have anywhere from 20 to 30 NSETS and maybe 10 to 15 KETs.

Because of the relaxed atmosphere of the villages – *fun*, the students will do nearly anything to enjoy themselves. Well, that's OK. Just go with it and you'll have fun, too. A friend of mine who once taught at a village once told me that student/teacher interaction was much better at the village, but nothing compared to the public school – better wage, less contact hours, more holidays, less management politics and teacher meetings.

You'll not be doing much "*real*" teaching. Most of what is asked of you is to entertain, role-play, and occasionally babysit the preschoolers.

ETIS (English Teachers in Seoul)
Seoul Metropolitan Office of Education (SMOE)

Well, long story short, this program has had its funding pulled, so I'm not going to comment on it other than to say that if indeed it does get funded, I'll do an update. Even so, I would not go into great detail regarding this program because it, too, is a near clone of the EPIK program.

Private Teaching/Tutoring

This venue is arguably the most desirable in Korea for obvious reasons. Before reading further, however, be aware that to teach this venue legally, only those who hold F series visas can do so. That said, you can make a very good living teaching privates. It is by far the most lucrative teaching gig in Korea.

If you live in the one of the larger Korean cities, you'll have no issues finding clients. I don't, but I still manage to do okay. Currently, 90 percent of my students are doctors at one of the larger hospitals, which means that the $60.00 to $70.00 per hour I charge them is chump change.

If you live in a smaller city, (less than 300,000) as I do, you'll really have to have a great PR gig going. Networking will become your best friend. And, yes, you'll want that PR kit, obviously.

If you find that things are slowing down, and you find yourself out of the comfort zone, you can always fire your PR kit to one of the many corporate recruiters in Seoul. These are the specialized recruiters whom I referred to earlier. They mostly hire for corporate English gigs, which means you'll be doing business/presentation English. They all, for the most part, have their own curricula, but of course you can deviate some.

They also pay very well and do have a few bonuses, albeit very small ones.

Also, you can contact the university language centers. I've gotten some real good gigs from the center, but the pay was much less than I normally charge.

I'll say no more on the subject because so few of you will be teaching privates.

Part Two

PARTICIPATING IN THE ENGLISH TEACHING MARKET

Chapter 10

Teaching Contracts

A little knowledge that acts is worth infinitely
more than much knowledge that is idle
- Khalil Gibran

Ah, contracts - the much misaligned **C** word. The first and most important thing to remember is that contracts, and this is true of many contract-challenged countries in Asia, are an entirely different animal. Once you've come to terms with this fact, you'll be better prepared when contract disputes arise. The primary difference between a Korean contract and a Western contract is that Korean contracts are traditionally based on verbal agreements, whereas in the West, contracts do not have this oral element; they are legally binding written documents that are based on the rule of law. They clearly demonstrate the obligations and responsibilities between parties.

I began with the aforementioned introduction because there seems no end to contract disputes in Korea. Western teachers mistakenly believe that Korean contracts follow the same rule of law that Western contracts do wherein there is little to no room for deviation of the clauses in that contract once it has been signed.

Many Western teachers in Korea also believe that a contract will save their asses in any dispute regarding said contract. This is sometimes the case, particularly if the teacher gets the attention and aid of the Korean Labor Board, but don't stake your job on it.

In a Korean contract, one's word was actually more important than any document. Just so, to bring themselves up to speed with globalization, Koreans have begun to use a Western style contract. Also, the details found in the contract are not nearly as important as verbal statements and understanding between parties. It's weird, I know. However, Korea and other Asian nations are *not* the West. Koreans value interpersonal relationships first and foremost and written documents second. Harmony, to the Korean, is at the heart of the matter.

More than a few directors, whether hagwon or not, might, after a certain amount of time, decide to deviate on the details of the contract. To the Korean, this is not an illegality; it is simply a necessity, and one's cooperation is expected. I have had this happen to me at nearly every venue in which I've taught. My experience has taught me that if the deviations were minor, I would simply roll with them. If they were major, well, I would negotiate up to a certain point. Keep in mind that all negotiation should include someone who can translate for you should you find that the director does not have the necessary English skills to make him/her understood to you, which often happens.

Moreover, teaching contracts, particularly at the hagown level, do vary in their wording. Many contracts are of the cut and paste variety – a little from this contract and a little from that. Not only that, I've found that the very same contract written in Korean differs on many points than the English translated contract. This is important because contracts written in Korean supersede the translated contract, so you will want be cautious when it comes to contracts. Know well that once you sign on the dotted line that you have just given up your rights to negotiate contracts points in your favor. Many folks come to Korea thinking, *"what the hell, if I don't like it, I'll simply resign and find another job."* This is not the case in Korea; the employer, should they agree with your resignation – and very few do – will have to give you a letter of release. Without the LOR, forget finding another job in Korea.

One of the red flags I found while browsing the Korean Labor Standards act was the fact that some smaller institutes may be exempt from all the provisions stated in the contract. If I'm correct, schools with less than four employees have a certain amount of contract leverage that larger schools do not have. I'll have to do more research into this to target just what those provisions are. What is important for you, oh potential NSET, is that when the shit hits the fan, as it is want to do, you may find negotiation impossible; therefore, you may want to reconsider signing a contract in an institute with a limited number of employees.

Let's have a look at a ten page EPIK contract. The EPIK program began in 1995, so the program is 18 years old. All contract issues have been pretty much ironed out, so it's a good contract. Long, yes, but reasonably safe should litigation arise, god forbid.

The sample contract is the actual contract used by EPIK. However, I've taken the liberty of removing most of the Korean script in the contract to save space and avoid confusion. This is a substantial contract, but we really need to analyze it for any flaws it might contain. It is also relevant because this is the very same contract you will be signing if you decide EPIK is for you. Naturally, I would have liked to present you with the full-size A4 copy, but it wasn't possible, given the space constraints of this book.

2 0 1 1 년 도 3 월 학 기 원 어 민 영 어 보 조 교 사 표 준 고 용 계 약 서 (안)
CONTRACT FOR March 2010 ENGLISH PROGRAM IN KOREA(EPIK)
교 육 과 학 기 술 부 국 립 국 제 교 육 원 EPIK (National EPIK)

대한민국 _____ 교육감(이하 "고용자"라 한다)과 _____ 국민인 원어민
(성명) _____ (이하 "피고용자"라 한다)은 대한민국의 원어민 영어보조교사
선발. 활용 사업을 위하여 다음과 같이 고용 계약을 체결한다.
This Contract of Employment (hereinafter referred to as "Contract") is made by and entered into
between the Superintendent of _____ Metropolitan/Provincial Office of Education,
(hereinafter referred to as "Employer"), and the Guest English Teacher (Name)
_____ (hereinafter referred to as "Employee") a citizen of
_____ .
- 고용기간 : 2011년 2월 26일 ~ 2012년 2월 25일
- Term of Employment : A one-year period from February 26, 2010 to February 25, 2011
- 고용등급 및 월급여 - Pay level and Salary
□ 1 등급/ 한화 _____ 원 □ 1 level/ _____ Korean Won per month
□ 2+등급/ 한화 _____ 원 □ 2+ level/ _____ Korean Won per month
□ 2 등급/ 한화 _____ 원 □ 2 level/ _____ Korean Won per month
□ 3 등급/ 한화 _____ 원 □ 3 level/ _____ Korean Won per month

Article 1 (Purpose) This contract sets forth the terms and conditions of employment for the Guest English Teacher's participation in the English Program in Korea.

Article 2 (Pay Level) ① The Employee shall be hired pursuant to this Contract with the Pay Level set forth at the beginning of this contract. ② The Pay Level set forth at the beginning of this Contract will be contingent upon provision of all the necessary documentational proof of qualifications and experience required by the Employer to be eligible for said Pay Level. ③ Any new qualifications obtained after the beginning of the Term of Employment will not subsequently change the Pay Level during the Term of Employment; the Pay Level will remain that agreed to at the beginning of the Term of Employment.

Article 3 (Duties) The Employee shall perform the following duties in the educational institutions of the undersigned Office of Education for the period indicated above: ① Assist Korean teachers with their English class(es) and/or jointly conduct English class(es) with

서명(Signature) -	고용자 (Employer) -	피고용자(Employee) -	피고용자(Employee)

Korean teachers,and/or lead extracurricular activities or English camps; ② Prepare teaching materials and lesson plans for English class(es); ③ Assist with the development and creation of teaching materials related to English language education; ④ Assist with activities related to English language education and other extracurricular activities such as but not limited to editing or creating English documents, judging contests, conducting teacher training, working at English camps, etc.; ⑤ Conduct English conversational class(es)/course(s) for Korean teachers and students; and ⑥ Perform other duties as designated by the Employer including various English programs during he school vacation period.

Article 4 (Supervision) The Employee shall carry out the duties set forth in the foregoing Article 3 pursuant to and under specific instruction and supervision of the Supervisor of the Work Place designated by Employer.

Article 5 (Term of Employment) ① The Term of Employment shall be the period set forth at the beginning of this Contract. ② If the Employee, for whatever reason, is unable to begin work on the date specified herein, the Contract shall be rewritten to indicate the new one year Term of Employment. The Contract will only take effect on the day the Employee is able to begin work and the Term of Employment shall be a one-year period beginning from that day forth. ③ This Term of Employment is not and shall not be considered a continuation of any previous Term of Employment with a different Office of Education. Hence, the Employer shall hire the GET as a new employee.

Article 6 (Resignation) ① The Employee shall perform the duties set forth under Article 3 hereof during the Term of Employment set forth under Article 5 hereof.
② This contract is binding unless the **Employee gives thirty (30) days written notice of termination** (stating a planned date of resignation and reason(s) therefore) to the principal of the Employee's main school as well as the Superintendent of the Office of Education.
③ Failure of the Employee to give thirty (30) days written notice of termination to the main school Principal and the Superintendent of the Office of Education shall be reported to the Korean Immigration Service and shall affect the Employee's ability to freely enter the Republic of Korea in the future.
④ In the case of the Employee's resignation his/her visa shall be canceled.

Article 7 (Work Place) ① **The Employee shall work at any location(s) designated by the Employer.** The location(s) designated by the Employer may include but are not limited to schools, Office of

서명(Signature) -	고용자 (Employer) -	피고용자(Employee) -	피고용자(Employee)

Education, training centers, or any other educational institutes located in the jurisdiction of the undersigned Office of Education.
② **The Employer may designate multiple locations for the Employee to work.**
③ The Employer may designate the Employee to work at the Office of Education, training centers or other educational institutes during the school vacation period. In this case, the Employee shall not claim for any additional pay if the hours of work fall under the regular Work Hours stated in Article 8.

Article 8 (Work Hours) ① **The Employee shall work eight (8) hours per day** for five (5) calendar days per week from Monday to

Friday and shall not work on Saturdays, Sundays and any national holidays of the Republic of Korea. **However, temporary English programs run by the Employer (e.g., English camp) may occur outside the Work Hours specified in this clause and on weekends.** In this case, the Employer shall pay according to Article 8, clause ③ and ④.

② The Work Hours of the Employee may follow the normal work schedule of civil servants of the Korean Government; however, such Work Hours may be adjusted by the Employer as he/she deems appropriate within the bounds set forth in Article 8, Clause ①.

③ **Actual class instruction hours of the Employee shall not exceed twenty-two (22) hours per week.** If, however, the Employee's actual weekly class instruction hours exceed twenty-two (22) hours due to supplementary class instruction, **the Employee shall be entitled to a supplementary class instruction pay of 20,000 won per hour.**

④ **The Employer may require the Employee to work non-instructional overtime hours in addition to normal** Work Hours. In this case, the Employee shall be entitled to supplementary overtime pay of 6,000 won per hour.

⑤ If the Employee agrees to teach instructional hours that occur outside the Work Hours specified in Article 8, clause ① and that total more than 22 hours per week, the Employer shall pay according to Article 8, clause ③. If the Employee agrees to teach instructional hours that occur outside the Work Hours specified in Article 8, clause ① but that total less than 22 hours per week, the Employer shall have the authority to determine the appropriate supplementary overtime pay.

Article 9 (Salary) ① The Employee shall be paid the amount set forth at the beginning of this Contract. However, the Korean income tax, residence tax, medical insurance premium, the national pension contribution, and any other tax or deduction mandated by the various levels of government shall be deducted each month from the Employee's salary.

② **The Employee's salary shall be paid on the 25th of the month.** If the 25th of the month falls on a Saturday, Sunday or a national holiday, the salary shall be paid on the immediately preceding

서명(Signature) -	고용자 (Employer) -	피고용자(Employee) -	피고용자(Employee)

business day.

③ If the Employee has not worked all of the normal working days in a month, for whatever reason (such as sick leave, unpaid leave, etc.), the Employee's salary for that month shall be prorated for the corresponding number of days worked.

④ If the Employee should be absent from work, for whatever reason, without having obtained prior approval from the Employer, the Employee's salary for that month shall be prorated according to the corresponding number of unauthorized absent days.

⑤ The Employee shall not claim against the Employer any compensation and/or payment other than those provided for in this Contract.

Article 10 (Renewal) ① The Term of Employment stated in Article 5 hereof may be renewed by the mutual written agreement of the Employer and the Employee provided that the renewal Term of Employment shall not exceed one (1) year.

② In the case of renewal of this Contract pursuant to the foregoing clause ①, the Employee shall be given two weeks paid leave which shall take place during the last two (2) calendar weeks prior to the end date specified under Article 5 hereof until the day immediately preceding the commencement of the renewed term. This two-week leave will be counted as part of the contract term, and, accordingly, salary will be paid as normal for these two weeks.

③ The Employer shall provide the Employee with a Contract Renewal Allowance of 2,000,000 Korean Won (KRW) within one month of the beginning of the new Term of Employment. In the case of Contract Renewal (and the payment of the subsequent Renewal Allowance), the GET shall not receive an Exit Allowance for the completion of the current Term of Employment nor shall the GET receive an Entrance Allowance for the renewal Term of Employment.

④ In case of the termination of the Renewal Contract within the first six (6) months, regardless of course or ground therefore, the Employee shall immediately pay back to the Employer 700,000 Korean Won (KRW) of the 2,000,000 Korean Won (KRW) Renewal Allowance.

Article 11 (Entrance Allowance/Exit Allowance) ① Upon beginning the Term of Employment, the Employee shall receive a 1,300,000 Korean Won (KRW) Entrance Allowance. The Entrance Allowance is not offered to Employees who are renewing their contract. For the first six (6) months of the Term of Employment, the Entrance Allowance of 1,300,000 Korean Won (KRW) shall be considered a loan to support the Employee's entrance into Korea. If the Employee receives a medical examination administered by EPIK, the cost of the medical examination shall be deducted from the 1,300,000 Korean Won (KRW) Entrance Allowance.

② In case of the termination of this Contract within the first six (6) months, regardless of course or ground therefore, the Employee shall immediately pay back to the Employer the aforementioned loan. Failure of the Employee to pay back the aforementioned loan shall be reported to the Korean Immigration Service and shall affect the Employee's ability to freely enter the Republic of

서명(Signature) -	고용자 (Employer) -	피고용자(Employee) -	피고용자(Employee)

Korea in the future. If the Employee successfully completes more than six (6) months of the Term of Employment from the date of commencement, the obligation of the Employee to pay back the Entrance Allowance loan shall be waived by the Employer.
③ If the Employee successfully completes his/her duties set forth in this contract for the full Term of Employment specified herein, **the Employee shall be entitled to an Exit allowance of 1,300,000 Korean Won (KRW) within one month of successful completion of the Term of Employment.**

Article 12 (Housing) ① **The Employer shall provide the Employee with a single housing chosen by the Employer.** Housing selected by the Employer may be a leased house, a studio-type room, an apartment, or other form of lodging deemed sufficient by the Employer. **Any and all fees, charges, costs, taxes, expenses, etc. incurred in using the housing shall be borne by the Employee. Such fees may include but are not limited to hydro, gas and water utilities as well as internet and phone service as well as a maintenance fee from the landlord.**
② The Employer may choose to provide temporary housing for the Employee until appropriate permanent housing can be obtained for the Employee.
③ If the Employee wants housing allowance in lieu of the single housing set forth in the foregoing ①, the Employer shall provide the Employee with 400,000 Korean Won (KRW) per month as a rent subsidy. In this case, the Employee shall notify the Employer of his/her decision to choose housing allowance before the commencement of this Contract.
④ The decision to choose the Provided Housing or the Housing Allowance shall be made prior to the beginning of the Term of Employment contained herein and, once decided, shall not be subsequently changed during the Term of Employment. Any and all costs incurred by the Employee as a result of changing Housing during the Term of Employment shall be borne by the Employee.
⑤ If the Employer provides housing to the Employee, **the Employer**

shall provide the following appliances and furniture: a bed, table and chair, a closet, a range, a refrigerator, a washing achine, and a TV set. The Employee shall not request or demand any other appliances or furniture than those stipulated herein.

⑥ If the Employee uses the housing provided by the Employer, the Employee shall leave the housing on the day after the final day of the contract.

⑦ If the Employee uses the housing provided by the Employer, the Employee shall leave the housing in the same condition as when it was first occupied and the Employee shall be liable for any damage to the building and appliances occurring during the period occupied by the Employee.

⑧ The Employer shall provide couples housing only to married couples jointly employed by the Employer. If the couple holds different last names, they must prove their marital status with a marriage certificate or other relevant documentation

서명(Signature) -	고용자 (Employer) -	피고용자(Employee) -	피고용자(Employee)

Article 13 (Benefits) ① The Employee shall be entitled to a one time Settlement Allowance of 300,000 Korean Won (KRW), when he/she first begins the contract. This Settlement Allowance will not be granted in the case of a Contract Renewal.

② On behalf of the Employee, **the Employer shall provide half of the Employee's medical insurance premium pursuant to the National Medical Insurance Act of Korea.** In the case of dependents of the Employee (spouse and/or children) living with him or her in Korea, the Employer shall also provide and pay the medical insurance premium for the Employee's dependents.

③ In the case that the Employees is working in a remote area (as designated by the undersigned Office of Education), the Employee may be eligible for a Rural Allowance of 100,000 Korean Won (KRW) per month. Designations for rural and non-rural areas are determined individually by the undersigned Office of Education.

④ In the case that the Employee is working at more than one school, the Employee shall receive a Multiple Schools Allowance of 100,000 Korean Won (KRW) for two schools or 150,000 Korean Won (KRW) for three or more schools per month.

⑤ Employees, with the exception of Canadians and Irish, shall be eligible for exemption from paying Korean income tax during the period of the first two years of Korean employment if they provide the following documents to the Employer before the first payment of salary: 1) "Residence Certificate" issued by the relevant authority of the

Employee's resident country 2) "an Application for Tax Exemption" on non-resident's Korean source income provided under the Korean Tax Treaty. If the Employee has already worked more than two years in Korea, he/she shall not be eligible for tax exemption.

⑥ **The Employer, on behalf of the Employee, shall provide half of the national pension plan deduction (approximately 4.5% of salary) pursuant to the National Pension Corporation Act** of Korea. American, Australian or Canadian Employees are eligible for a pension distribution refund if they submit the required documents to the Korean National Pension Corporation when they leave Korea after the completion of their Contract.

⑦ **The Employee shall be entitled to severance pay according to the standard formula set out by the Ministry of Labor (equivalent to approximately one month's salary), upon successful completion of the duties set out under Article 3 hereof for the entire Term of Employment set out at the beginning of the Contract.**

⑧ The Employer may provide a special allowance to an employee who has made a great contribution to the Employer and/or who is determined to work at a special institute by the Employer.

서명(Signature) -	고용자 (Employer) -	피고용자(Employee) -	피고용자(Employee)

Article 14 (Paid Leave) ① **The Employee shall be entitled to a vacation period of a total of eighteen (18) working days** during the Term of the Employment set forth under Article 5 hereof. If the Employees works in a school, **the Employee shall have vacation for eight (8) working days during the summer recess and ten (10) working days during the winter recess respectively**; If the Employee works in a training center, the Employee shall have their vacation outside the normal training session times. If the requested vacation period interferes with the smooth operation of the programming of the school or institute, the Employer and the Employee shall negotiate an alternate vacation date(s).

② The Employee shall apply for and obtain the Employer's consent to take any paid leave a minimum of fifteen (15) calendar days in advance of the requested date of leave.

③ The Employee shall note the difference between school vacation and Paid Vacation days; the Employee is expected to fulfill normal working duties during the school vacation period unless the Employee has received prior approval for Paid Vacation or Unpaid Leave during the school vacation period.

④ Regardless of the number of days over which the Paid Leave falls, eight (8) accumulated hours of Paid Leave shall be counted as one day.

This includes tardiness, early leave, other absences during the work day and/or half-days of Paid Leave. A total of less than eight (8) hours will not be counted.

Article 15 (Sick Leave) ① The Employee shall be entitled to a paid Sick Leave in the case of any illness or injury which prevents the Employee from performing the duties herein only with the express consent of the Employer. The Employee shall notify the Employer of any absence due to sickness within one (1) hour of the beginning of the Employee's duties.

② **The Employee's paid Sick Leave during the Term of Employment shall not exceed eleven (11) working days.** Regardless of whether the sick-leave days are consecutive or individual, the Employee shall not require a doctor's note for the first three (3) days of sick leave taken during the Term of Employment. However, a practicing doctor's medical report shall be required for any sick-leave periods taken above the three-day threshold, whether these days are consecutive or individual. The time period of the sick leave must not exceed the period advised by the physician's report. Letters from a physician must be submitted to the Employer on the first day that the Employee returns to the work place.

③ If the Employee requires a Sick Leave of more than eleven (11) working days during the Term of Employment, any working days beyond the 11-day limit will be unpaid.

④ The total number of days of Sick Leave (both paid and unpaid) used by the Employee and the reasons for taking Sick Leave will be included in the Employee's Personnel Record Card, which shall be utilized by the Employer to evaluate the Employee's conduct and determine the Employee's contract renewal.

Article 16 (Special Leave) ① The Employee may take a paid Special Leave for a number of days as set forth below for each of the following events stated herein only with the express consent of the Employer:
1. Seven (7) calendar days for the Employee's marriage.
2. Seven (7) calendar days for the death of an Employee's parent or spouse; five (5) calendar days

서명(Signature) -	고용자 (Employer) -	피고용자(Employee) -	피고용자(Employee)

for the death of an Employee's child.
3. In case of a female Employee, ninety (90) calendar days shall be granted for a maternity leave. In the case of maternity leave, only the

first 60 days shall be paid leave; the last 30 days shall be unpaid leave.

Article 17 (Codes of Conduct) ① The Employee shall not behave in any manner which may damage or tarnish the reputation of the teaching profession in general or of the EPIK program and the undersigned Employer in particular.

② The Employee shall observe and comply with any codes of conduct and dress applicable to Korean teachers.

③ The Employee shall not engage in any other employment (including any part-time, private or self-employment, or online instruction) during the Term of Employment set forth under Article 5 hereof.

④ The Employee shall not be involved in any activity which could cause harm to the students or be of detriment to the reputation of the school.

⑤ Employees must not disclose any confidential information about their co-workers, school or program that they have acquired during their term of employment.

Article 18 (Termination of the Contract) ① The Employer may legally terminate or cancel this Contract upon occurrence of any one or more of the following events:

1. The Employee violates the laws of the Republic of Korea.

2.   The Employee works in Korea without holding the required valid visa.

3.   The Employee fails to perform or unsatisfactorily performs any of the duties stipulated in this contract. The Employer shall provide formal written notice of unsatisfactory performance to the Employee. Three or more written notices shall be considered sufficient grounds for Termination of the Contract.

4. The Employee engages in any other employment (including any part-time, private or self-employment, or online instruction) during the Term of Employment set forth under Article 5 herein.

5. The Employee fails to perform his/her duties for more than five working days without receiving prior consent from the Employer.

서명(Signature) -	고용자 (Employer) -	피고용자(Employee) -	피고용자(Employee)

6. Any of the information provided in the Employee's application is neither true nor accurate.

7. It is determined that the Employee is prevented from or incapable of performing the duties set forth under Article 3 hereof for any medical

reason, whether it is physical or psychological in nature, including chronic ailments such as diabetes Mellitus, high blood pressure, chronic liver disease, tuberculosis, neurologic disorder, substance or alcohol addiction, etc.

a. If requested to take a physical and/or psychological examination by the Employer, the Employee must make themselves available within two (2) working days for the medical examination.

b. The Employee must complete a medical examination (HIV, Drug etc) in Korea for the purpose of working in Korean public schools and educational institutions. If requested by the Employer, the Employee must submit the results to the Employer immediately.

8. The total number of days of sick leave (both paid and unpaid) used by the Employee pursuant to Article 15 hereof exceeds thirty (30) days.

② **In the event of termination of this Contract pursuant to any of the provisions set forth in the foregoing clause ①, the Employer shall pay the Employee a prorated salary for the final month of work based on the number of days actually worked by the Employee.**

③ In the event of termination of this Contract pursuant to any of the provisions set forth in the foregoing clause ①, the Employee shall immediately refund the loan to the Employer pursuant to Article 11①.

④ In such event, the Employer will not pay the Employee the Exit Allowance. The Employee's visa will subsequently be cancelled.

Article 19 (Completion of Mandatory Orientation and Training) ①
The Employee shall complete all training deemed necessary by EPIK and/or the undersigned Office of Education. This includes but is not limited to an orientation held before the beginning of the Term of Employment and/or in-service training during the Term of Employment.

② The Employee will not be entitled to compensation for any portion of the mandatory orientation which falls outside the Term of Employment as stipulated under Article 5.

③ The Employee shall participate in any training program(s) upon request of the Employer.

Article 20 (Indemnification) The Employee hereby agrees to indemnify, defend and hold harmless the Employer against any and all liability, claims, suits, losses, costs and legal fees caused by, arising out of or resulting from any negligent, intentional or illegal act of the Employee during the Term of Employment under this Contract.

Article 21 (Consent to Limited Release of Information) The Employee grants his/her consent that the information in the Employee's

137

application form and/or Personnel Record Card may be used for the purpose of statistical data collected by the Employer and/or the Korean government, for his/her contract renewal with his/her current Employer or his/her new application to other provinces.

Article 22 (Governing Law, Language and Venue) (1) The terms of this Contract and the rights and obligations of the parties hereto shall be construed, interpreted and determined in accordance with

서명(Signature) -	고용자 (Employer) -	피고용자(Employee) -	피고용자(Employee)

the laws of the Republic of Korea.
(2) The Governing language of the Contract shall be Korean. The English translation of this Contract is offered for the purpose of convenience only.
(3) If a dispute or disagreement should arise in connection with or out of this Contract, the parties hereto shall first try to resolve it in accordance with the principle of good faith. If the parties fail to mutually resolve such disputes or disagreements or come to amicable settlements, their disputes or disagreements shall be resolved by arbitration in Seoul, Korea in accordance with the Commercial Arbitration Rules of the Korean Commercial Arbitration Board.
(4) Matters not explicitly stated in the Contract shall be determined by the Employer by taking the Employee's concerns into consideration.

Article 23 (Signature) In witness whereof, the parties hereto sign the Contract in triplicate on the date entered below with each party retaining one copy and submitting the third copy for the Employee's visa application.

(Author's note: contract continued on the next page)

서명일 (Dated): 2011 . . .

고용자 (Employer's signature)	피고용자 (Employee's signature)
성명 (Name) 직책 (Position):	성명 (Name)

서명(Signature) -	고용자 (Employer) -	피고용자(Employee) -	피고용자(Employee)

Indeed, a fairly comprehensive contract. Next, let's have a look at what your contract should contain, and examine each point for contract point fulfillment. I've given the article number in bold print where readers will find each point.

- Try to get your exact scheduled work hours listed in the contract. **Article 8. Partially fulfilled. Read the chapter on EPIK.**
- Try to get the exact date of payment to be a specific day every month, i.e. "The employee will be paid on the 10th of every month, or if pay day falls on a weekend or holiday, the closest preceding work day." **Article 9. Fulfilled**

- If you start in the middle of the month, make sure your contract states you will have the properly prorated salary for the first month. **EPIK NSETs rarely, if ever, begin in the middle of the month, so this point is moot.**
- It is highly discouraged that you accept work on Saturdays more than several times a year for special events. Six day work weeks will wear you down. **Article 8. EPIK NSETs almost never teach on Saturdays. Just so, there are special programs that you may be asked to teach during the weekends.**
- It is highly discouraged that you pay housing deposits in the beginning of your contract. The reasons for these deposits are numerous, but essentially, it is insurance for the hagwon against you leaving early. Do not expect to see this money again if you accept a contract with deposits. **EPIK contracts do not require housing deposits.**
- Housing should be single and private. Do not accept shared housing. Sharing an apartment with another person for a year can turn into a nightmare. **Article 12. Fulfilled**
- Housing should be paid for in full by the school. Utilities, maintenance and internet are paid by the employee. **Article 12. Fulfilled**
- Your housing should list what amenities you are to receive. The most important is that you have a bed and an air conditioner. An air conditioner is a necessity in Korea, where summers get incredibly hot and the humidly becomes

unbearable. A basic wall mount air conditioner costs around 400,000 won – about $380.00. **Article 12. Partially fulfilled. No A.C**

- Overtime should be a minimum of 20,000 won per hour. **Article 8. Fulfilled**
- Forced overtime is illegal. A contract that states you may have to work more hours than the stated amount is illegal. **Article 8. Gray area here. EPIK NSETs may be required to work additional hours over base. However, they are compensated for those hours**
- Working at more than one location is legal as an E-2 visa holder, as long as it is listed on your ARC (Alien Registration Card) and is a location sponsored by the same employer. **Article 7. EPIK NSETs may be farmed out to other government locations. This is legal.**
- Three paid sick days is standard. A doctor's note is generally required. **Article 15. Fulfilled**
- Ten vacation days is the standard, usually broken into two blocks of five days. Be sure that you can take your vacation days when you want; don't let the hagwon schedule them for you. This can lead to overlapping with national holidays, which the school might still count as your personal vacation. **Article 14.Fulfilled**
- All national holidays need to be days off, and paid as regular. **No mention of this. However, I personally know that point is fulfilled**
- Severance must be given upon the completion of a contract, equal to one month's salary.

Failure to complete your contract will result in not receiving severance. **Article 13. Fulfilled**.

- You must be enrolled in the NHIC health insurance plan. This is a government program. All E-2 visa holders must be registered for it, regardless of what anyone says. The cost/premium should be 2.67 percent of your salary, half of which is paid by the school. Do not, under any circumstances, accept private health insurance. **Article 13. Partially fullfiled – no mention of premium.**

- Similarly, you are also legally required to be enrolled in the national pension program. Don't worry, you will get it back unless you are from South Africa or the UK. The pension should be 4.5 percent of your salary, with your employer matching it with another 4.5 percent. Failure to include this in your contract is not only illegal, but also cheating you out of $400-500 dollars a year. **Article 13. Fulfilled**

- 30 days is the standard amount of time you need to be notified if you are being laid off, and you must receive either one month's pay if immediately laid off, or a 30 day working period, wherein you will receive a full month's salary at the end. **This is the law. Article 18. Partially fulfilled. No mention of a 30 day notification.**

- 30 days is also the standard amount of time that you should give before resigning or leaving before the contract is over. **Article 6. Fulfilled**

- Airfare should be provided and paid in full at the beginning and end of your contract, paid for or fully reimbursed by the school. **No mention of this in the contract. However, I know this to be fulfilled.**

- After six months, you should not be required to pay back your airfare to Korea. Some contracts say one year, but six months is the standard. **Not fulfilled.**

Next is a standard contract used by most hagwons.

SAMPLE

Employment Contract

Position: English Language Instructor

EMPLOYER	EMPLOYEE
Name of School:	Employee's Name:
Address:	Address:
(Hereafter to be referred to as the Employer)	(Hereafter to be referred to as the Employee)

The Parties agree as follows:

(Author's note: continued on the next page)

I.	**TERM OF CONTRACT**	
	1.	This contract will be valid for a period of 12 months beginning _____ and ending _____

II.	**EMPLOYEE REQUIREMENTS**	
	1	The Employee will act in an appropriately professional manner and be responsible for conducting professional English Language classes.
	2.	The Employee will be required to work for regularly scheduled hours from Monday through Friday (In a special case like lunar new year or Choosuk holiday, one of the Saturdays or a national holiday in the month which includes a Korean traditional holiday can be exchanged with a weekday off to secure the convenience of the students and their parents), 30 hours of teaching per week, or a total of 120 hours of teaching per a month. The Employee will be required to come to the campus 40 minutes prior to class starting time.
	3.	The Employee is required to attend the events held by The Employer such as workshops, year ending party, retreats, academic seminars, etc.

III.	**SERVICES PROVIDED BY THE EMPLOYER**	
	1.	**PAYMENT**
		1.1	The Employer will pay a monthly salary of _____ won for regularly scheduled hours.
		1.2	The Employer will pay a monthly salary of _____ won in the event that the Employer is unable to provide the Employee with the regularly scheduled 120 hours per month.
		1.3	If the Employee fails to work the regularly scheduled hours due to tardiness, absence, etc.; the monthly payment will be calculated and paid using a daily rate and/or an hourly rate. The method of calculating daily rate: Monthly salary divided by 30. The method of calculating hourly rate: Daily rate divided by 6.
		1.4	The Employer may ask the Employee to work over time (the Employee is expected to cooperate to supply better service to his or her students), and if the Employee chooses to do overtime, the Employer will pay for the overtime at the rate of _____ won per hour.
		1.5	The Employer will pay a monthly salary or the total sum of amount for one full month of work on the 30th of the each month. In the case the employee doesn't start working on the very first day of the month his/ her working days for the month will be counted from the day when he/ she started working a regular

2.		HOUSING
	2.1	The Employer will provide the Employee a single apartment or one room in a safe environment with certain furniture items (bed, washing machine, gas range, refrigerator, TV, a table suitable for taking meals, fan or air conditioner, some utensils and cookware) and the apartment will be provided at no cost to the Employee with the exception of utilities and phone bills.
	2.2	The employee should have the duty preserving the housing and the furniture items provided by the employer until the termination of this contract. If they are destroyed, the employee should restore them to the original state or pay the cost needed in purchasing the same level of the substitutes of them.
	2.3	The employer will deduct 200,000won from each of the employee's first three months of pay to make a total of 600,000won as a housing management deposit. This deposit is to cover any unpaid monthly service or utility bills in the event the employee fails to pay for any service or goods which she/he used throughout the contract. The employer will hold the full amount of the deposit until all payable bills are checked to have been paid.
3.		AIRFARE
	3.1	A round-trip airfare (standard economy ticket) from the Employee's designated city to Korea before departure will be provided only for the Employee who will be fulfilling a 12-month period and who has been hired outside of Korea. This is not applicable if hired within Korea. If the employee leaves the school before six (6) months, the employee must payback the initial airfare or the employer may deduct the amount of airfare from the teacher's last payment
	3.2	In the event when the airfare is paid by the Employee him/herself before departure, the airfare will be reimbursed by the Employer to the employee after the issuance of an E-2 Visa from Korean Immigration Office. The reimbursement is subject only to the Employee who will be fulfilling a 12-month of employment period and has been hired outside of Korea. This is not applicable if hired within Korea.
4.		LODGING
	4.1	The Employer will provide lodging, if necessary, for the Employee's stay for the orientation and training period at a facility provided by the Employer.
5.		HEALTH PLAN
	5.1	The Employer will pay 50% of the premium for the Employee's health plan, which is provided by the Employer and are administered through the Employer (Participation in a health plan is optional, But it will be mandatory from year 2006). The Employee will be responsible for rest of the costs.
6.		SEVERANCE PAY
	6.1	The Employer will pay severance to the Employee upon completion of contract. The amount of the severance pay will be the same of a month salary(won), and if necessary, applicable government deductions will be subtracted.
7.		PAID VACATION
	7.1	The Employee may use 8 working days as paid vacation per year. Three days of Institute-scheduled vacation are counted in these 8 days. None of these 8 days may be taken during the first three months of employment. The remaining 5 days must be scheduled with the Institute at least one month in advance. (5 days out of

			8 days has to be used in official break period of Institute.) Days in which the Employee does not regularly work i.e., Saturdays, Sundays and National Holidays are not to be considered as part of the vacation period.	
		7.2	The Employee will be paid for all national holidays and not be expected to work during these days otherwise in special occasion for which Employee agrees to work voluntarily.	
	8.	**SICK DAY**		
		8.1	The Employee may use up to 3 paid sick days per year with the doctor's note from a company-designated hospital, and after the 5 sick days have been used, it will be counted as absent and the pay will be calculated according to the Daily Rate/Hourly Rate.	
		8.2	No more than two consecutive sick days may be taken at once.	
	9.	**PENSION**		
			The Employee and the Institute will make regular contributions to the Employee's pension fund, as stipulated by the rules and regulations of Korean National Pension Corporation. If eligible, the Employee will receive a reimbursement of all contributions made by him/herself and the Institute upon departure from Korea.	
IV.	**RENEWAL & TERMINATION OF CONTRACT**			
	1.	**RENEWAL**		
		1.1	The Employee must give the Employer a written 45-day notice before renewal or non-renewal of the Employee's current contract.	
		1.2	Both the Employer and the Employee reserve the option to renew the contract.	
	2.	**TERMINATION OF CONTRACT**		
		2.1	Both parties will give at least a written 45-day notice prior to the termination date of the contract.	
		2.2	The Employer retains the right to terminate the contract immediately if:	
			a.	The Employee is unable to discharge the responsibilities or meet the conditions such as being late for class on a continuous basis; continuous failure to keep regularly scheduled working hours and repeated absences from classes without a valid reason.
			b.	The Employee teaches off the Employer's property.
			c.	The Employee uses illegal drugs or is intoxicated during work hours.
			d.	The Employee participates in any type of criminal activity of corruption of public moral that violates the laws of the Republic of South Korea.
			e.	The Employee receives 3 times of written notice from the Employer.
			f.	The employee tells the others about his/ her own employment contract details.
		2.3	If, for any reason, the contract is terminated before the full completion of the contract period:	
			a.	The Employee will not qualify for benefits such as severance pay and the airfares.
			b.	The Employee will be wholly responsible for any utilities/maintenance and phone bills remaining for the duration of their housing lease.
		2.4	Within 14-days the Employee is required to sign a notice of termination and accompany the employer to the Korean Immigration office to notify the Korean	

V.		VENUE FOR DISPUTES BETWEEN EMPLOYER AND EMPLOYEE
	1.	The appropriate laws of the Republic of Korea will govern this contract. However, while both parties enter into this agreement with total honesty and integrity, disputes may sometimes occur. In such cases, both parties will be bound by all terms and conditions of this contract and will try to resolve the difference in a civil manner that is fair to both parties. In the event that no solution can be found for a problem and either party decides to terminate this contract, they must do so in accordance with Section IV, 2 above. Upon such termination, both parties will agree to remain civil and to speak honestly and fairly about their experiences and not in a disrespectful manner.
VI.		FULL KNOWLEDGE
	1.	GOOD FAITH
		The Employer and the Employee will act in good faith toward each other. The Employer will not dismiss the Employee without what reasonably is considered good cause and the Employee will do their utmost to satisfactorily fulfill all the responsibilities and meet all the conditions as described in the above agreement.
	2.	CHANGES TO CONTRACT
		The Employer and the Employee agree that they have read the entirety of this Employment Contract and no other verbal agreement, statement or promise made on or before the effective date of this contract will be binding on the parties. Any changes made must be in writing and signed by both parties to be included in this contract. Any changes made to this contract, whether verbal or other, without the knowledge and written consent of both parties are to be considered invalid, and as such are not parts of this contract.
	3.	TRANSFERAL OF CONTRACT
		Under no circumstances can the Employer exchange, give, sell, or transfer this contract or the services of the Employee to another party or Institute without the written consent of the Employee.
	4.	LANGUAGE OF CONTRACT
		The language of this contract is written in English. For convenience of the employer this contract may be translated into Korean upon request and prior to the signing of this document. In event of a dispute, the English version of this contract will prevail.
VII		ADDITIONS TO CONTRACT
		All other matters not stated above will be based on Korean relevant laws and regulations including The labor standard Act, Regulations about employment and Avalon company regulations. When the employee is temporarily required to work in the head office by the employer, for reasons such as curriculum development, the working hours are 10am~7pm and there will be a one hour lunch break.

Employee:_____
Date:_____
Employer:_____
Date:_____
Director of:_____

You homework is to analyze this contract and see what points found within need further clarification.

With this type of contract, you must be on the watch for too many punitive clauses (actions intended to punish people). These clauses are there for many reasons, and those reasons are usually not in your best interest. If you find that a contract has many punitive clauses – more than what's normal – you will probably want to walk away from the job offer. These clauses are a clue as to what kind of hagwon you're getting involved with. Many clauses normally mean that the hagwon has had problems with teachers; which may or may not be the teacher's fault.

Chapter 11

Lesson Plans

—To plan or not to plan...

I believe it is very important that you have knowledge about the format of a typical Korean lesson plan because it differs from its Western counterpart. Moreover, you may not have had any previous experience with lesson planning during your ESL/EFL certification program training. So, forewarned is forearmed.

You may or may not have to do your own lesson plan. It depends on your KET; some are incredibly lazy and will tell you that you're on your own, while others are more helpful and will contribute to a lesson plan. Be prepared for both scenarios. EPIK KETs and KETs from other government programs will probably have to do lesson plans because it is one of the articles in the contract.

So, without further ado, here's a sample for your perusal:

Master Plan

1. Unit: Lesson 3: Where? Who did it?

2. General Objectives: to introduce past progressive using authentic language

3. Specific Objective:

1) Functional Skills: Students will learn the following

- Proverb "A rolling stone gathers no moss"

- Answer the question "Who hurt you?"

- Express sympathy "I'm sorry to hear that"

2) Language Skills: The students will learn the following,

- Verb tense ex. Kick/kicked, come/came, feel/felt

- Describe ongoing past activities.

4. Teaching Aids:

-PowerPoint, Worksheet, Illustrations

5. Sub Plan-Speaking Activity

Unit	Lesson 5: Where? Who did it?	Instructors	Perry Como & Se Yeong Jeong	Class 1-1
Date	08/11/12			Period 3/5

Learning Objective	Students will be able to: 1) Add a proverb to their proverb portfolio 2) Use past progressive tense 3) Be able to answer "who did it?"

Teaching Aids	PowerPoint, Worksheets, Illustrations

Teaching Plan

Flow Chart: ○- Whole class ●-Individual work ◐- Pair work

STEPS	Flow Chart	Procedure	Activities Teacher	Activities Student	Time	Aids
INTRODUCTION	○ ○ ○ ○	Greeting and current events	- Hello class - Ask about Sports Day	- Greet teacher - respond to the question	5min	
		Review	- review former proverb. - introduce the new proverb. "A rolling stone gathers no moss"	- review the expression - listen and repeat	5min	-PPT -VIS
		Present this weeks learning objective.	- present past tense and past progressive tense.	- listen		-PPT

152

D E V E L O P M E N T	o	Warm up Introduce past progressive expression	- introduce verbs and their corresponding past tense.	- participate	10min	-PPT -VIS
	o					
	o	Introduce the past progressive sentence form.	- where were you when it began to rain?	-listen and repeat		-PPT
	o		- use example of Mike playing baseball.	- participate and answer		
	•	Assign Class work	- demonstrate using two examples.			
		Check comprehension		- Students work together and complete the assigned conversations.	10min	- HO
			- choose 2 students to present their answers.	- present finished answers		
		Introduce the "while- clause"				
			- provide proper feedback.			
			- Teachers present a role play	- listen and respond	10min	-PPT -HO
C O N S O L I D A T I O N	o	Review	- ask for today's proverb	- respond	5min	-PPT
		Summarize past progressive	- highlight the three steps to make a past progressive sentence.			-HO
	•	Assign homework	- finish 'why what happened' and be prepared to present next class.			

153

Co-Teaching Lesson Plan

Who did it?

Where?

School	Gunsan Middle School
Teachers	Perry Romo, Se Yeong Jeon
Subject	English 6
Unit	Lesson 3: Where? Who did it?
Date	08/11/12
Class	1-1 (Orange class)

Chapter 12

Sample Documents

—Here a document, there a document...

Sample documents include:

1. Apostille, Criminal Record Check, and where to find the proper authentication office in your state,   province, or country

2. E-2 Visa Health Statement

3. Visa Application Form

Criminal Record Check & Apostille Information

The Ministry of Justice of Korea requires all foreign teacher applicants to submit apostilled, state-level criminal record checks. Under the international apostille agreement, all applicants from US, UK, NZ, SA, IR, AU can obtain the apostille stamp from designated authorities. Canadian applicants must get their CRCs notarized at the nearest Korean Embassies/Consulates.

155

Australia

Department of Foreign Affairs and Trade
2nd Floor, R.G. Casey Building, John McEwen
Crescent, Barton, ACT, 0221
Tel: 02 6261 1111
Email: consular.feedback@dfat.gov.au
Price: AUD $60 per Apostille certificate
http://www.dfat.gov.au/

Canada

Korean Embassies/Consulates located in Canada

Montreal	Toronto
1 Place Ville Marie Suite 2015 Montreal, Quebec Canada H3B 2C4 (514) 845-3243/44	555 Avenue Road, Toronto, Ontario M4V 2J7 (416)920-3809
Vancouver	Korean Embassy
1600-1090 West Georgia St. Vancouver, BC V6E 3V7 (604) 685-9577	150 Boteler Street Ottawa Ontario, K1N 5A6 (613)244-5010

Ireland

The Department of Foreign Affairs
Consular Section
Department of Foreign Affairs 69 - 71 Hainault House St.
Stephen's Green DUBLIN 2

Telephone: +353 1 408 2174 / +353 1 408 2322
Website: www.dfa.ie

Department of Foreign Affairs-Consular Services
1a South Mall
CORK
Telephone: +353 21 494 4777 / Fax: +353 21 494 4772

Price: € 20 for each Apostille.
Useful Links: http://www.dfa.ie/home/index.aspx?id=268

New Zealand

[Important Note] Police clearance or background checks can be sent straight to the Authentication Unit, unless the document is computer generated, in which case it will need to be notarized first by a Notary Public.

Department of Internal Affairs, Authentication Unit

By Courier
Authentication Unit, Level 13, Prime Property Tower, 86-90 Lambton Quay, Wellington 6011, NZ

By Standard post
Authentication Unit (c/o The Translation Service), PO Box 805, Wellington 6140, NZ
Telephone: +64 (4) 470 2928 / Fax: +64 (4) 470 2921
E-mail: authentication@egs.govt.nz
Contact person: Carlee Reid
Website: http://www.dia.govt.nz/apostille

Price: NZD $40 per Apostille certificate

NZD $15 per copy Certificate (Apostille of identical document / same issuing authority)

Useful Links: http://www.dia.govt.nz/apostille

South Africa

Any registrar or assistant registrar of the Supreme Court of South Africa:

Physical Address
Constitutional Court, Constitution Hill (cnr Queen- and Sam Hancock/Hospital Streets), BRAAMFONTEIN

Postal Address

Constitutional Court, Constitution Hill, Private Bag X1,
BRAAMFONTEIN 2017
Telephone: +27 (11) 403-8032 / +27 (11) 359-7460
Fax: +27 (11) 403-6524

Department of Justice

Postal address
Private Bag X81, PRETORIA, 0001, Momentum Centre,
329 Pretorius Street (c/o Pretorius and Prinsloo Streets)
PRETORIA, SA
Telephone: +27 (12) 315 1111
Fax: +27 (12) 357 1112
General website: http://www.doj.gov.za

Department of Foreign Affairs
Postal address
Private Bag X152, PRETORIA 0001, SA

Pretoria address
East Wing, Union Building, Government Ave, Arcadia,
PRETORIA

Cape Town address
120 Plein Street, Parliamentary Precinct, CAPE TOWN
Telephone: Pretoria office +27 (12) 351 1000
Cape Town office + 27 (21) 464 3700
Fax: Pretoria office +27 (12) 351 0165

E-mail: info@foreign.gov.za
Website: http://www.dfa.gov.za

United Kingdom of Great Britain and Northern Ireland
Legalisation Office
Foreign &Commonwealth Office
Old Admiralty Building, The Mall, LONDON SW1A 2LG
The DX number: The Legalisation Office, DX 123243, St
James' Park

Telephone: +44 (20) 7008 1111
E-mail: LegalisationOffice@fco.gov.uk
Contact person: Mr James Evans, Legalisation Office
Manager
Price: £ 27 for each Apostille.
http://www.fco.gov.uk

United States of America
Apostille offices will only certify documents issued in that
state and fees vary by state.

State Authentication Authorities

Alabama Apostille - Authentication Offices
Designated Authority: Secretary of State *Alabama*
Office of the Secretary of State
Authentication Section
State Capitol, Room E-204
600 Dexter Ave.
Montgomery, AL 36104
334-242-7210
http://www.sos.state.al.us/authenticate/index.htm

Fee: $5.00

Alaska Apostille - Authentication Offices
Designated Authority: Secretary of State *Alaska*
Notary Administrator
Office of the Lieutenant Governor
P.O. Box 110015
Juneau, AK 99811- 0015
907-465-3509
http://www.gov.state.ak.us/ltgov/notary/authentications.
htm

Fee: $2.00

Arizona Apostille - Authentication Offices
Designated Authority: Lieutenant Governor; Attorney
General; Clerk of the Supreme Court *Arizona*

Office of the Secretary of State
Business Services Division, Notary Section
1700 W. Washington, 7th Floor
Phoenix, AZ 85007-2888
602 542-4086/ 602 542-4758
http://www.sosaz.com/notary

Fee: $3.00

Arkansas Apostille - Authentication Offices
Designated Authority: Secretary of State; Assistant
Secretary of State. *Arkansas*
Office of Secretary of State
Corporations Division
State Capitol
Little Rock, AR 72201-1094
501-682-3409
http://www.sosweb.state.ar.us/business.html

Fee: $10.00

California Apostille - Authentication Offices
Designated Authority: Secretary of State; Chief Deputy
Secretary of State. *California*
Office of the Secretary of State
Business Programs Division
Notary Public Section
P.O. Box 942877
Sacramento, CA 94277-0001
916-653-3595
http://www.ss.ca.gov/business/notary/notary.htm

Fee: $20.00

Colorado Apostille - Authentication Offices
Designated Authority: Secretary of State; any Assistant
Secretary of State; any

Deputy Secretary of State. *Colorado*
Office of Secretary of State
1700 Broadway, Suite 300
Denver, CO 80202
303-894-2300 ext 6409
http://www.sos.state.co.us/pubs/info_center/2001fees.ht
m

Fee: By Mail: FREE | While You Wait: $15.00

Connecticut Apostille - Authentication Offices
Designated Authority: Secretary of State; Deputy Secretary
of State. *Connecticut*
30 Trinity St.
Hartford, CT 06106
860-509-6135
http://www.sots.state.ct.us/recordslegislativeservices/aut
hen.html#orders

Fee: $20.00

Delaware Apostille - Authentication Offices
Designated Authority: Secretary of State; Deputy Secretary
of State. *Delaware*
Office of Secretary of State
Notary Division
401 Federal St., Suite 3
Dover, DE 19901
302- 302/739-4111
http://www.state.de.us/sos/sos.htm

Fee: $10.00

**District of Columbia Apostille - Authentication
Offices**

Designated Authority: Secretary of State; Acting Secretary of State. ***District of Columbia***
Office of the Secretary, D.C.

Notary Commissions & Authentications Section
441 4th St. N.W. (One Judiciary Square)
Washington, D.C.
202-727-3117
http://os.dc.gov/info/notary/notary.shtm#document

Fee: $10.00
Designated Authority: Executive Secretary; Assistant Executive Secretary; Mayor's Special Assistant and Assistant to the Executive Secretary; Secretary of the District of Columbia.

Florida Apostille - Authentication Offices
Designated Authority: Department of State - ***Florida***
Department of State
Office of International Affairs
Notary Certification/Apostille Section
The Capitol Building
Suite 1902
Tallahassee, FL 32399-0250
804-488-7521
http://notaries.dos.state.fl.us/notproc7.htm

Fee: $10.00

Georgia Apostille - Authentication Offices
Designated Authority: Secretary of State ***Georgia***
Georgia Superior Court Clerks" Cooperative Authority
Notary Division
1875 Century Boulevard, Suite 100
Atlanta, GA 30345
404-327-6023
http://www.gsccca.org/Projects/apost.asp or Office of Secretary of State
Administrative Procedures Unit

2 Martin Luther King Jr. Drive
Suite 820 - West Tower
Atlanta, Georgia 30334404-656-2885

http://www.gsccca.org/Projects/apost.asp

Fee: $3.00

Hawaii Apostille - Authentication Offices
Designated Authority: Secretary of State; Georgia Superior
Court Clerks" Cooperative Authority. *Hawaii*
Office of the Lieutenant Governor
State Capitol, 5 th Floor,
Honolulu, Hawaii 96813
808-586-0255
http://www.state.hi.us/ltgov/page8.html

Fee: $1.00
Designated Authority: Lieutenant Governor of the State of
Hawaii.

Idaho Apostille - Authentication Offices
Designated Authority: Secretary of State - *Idaho*
Office of Secretary of State
Notary Department
Box 83720
Boise, ID 83720
208- 332-2810
http://www.idsos.state.id.us/notary/apostill.htm
Fee:$10.00

Illinois Apostille - Authentication Offices
Designated Authority: Secretary of State; Chief Deputy
Secretary of State; Deputy Secretary of State; Notary Public
Clerk. *Illinois*
Office of the Secretary of State
Index Department, Notaries Public Division
111 E. Monroe St.
Springfield, IL 62756

217- 217-782-7017
http://www.sos.state.il.us/departments/index/division.ht
ml

Fee: $2.00

Indiana Apostille - Authentication Offices
Designated Authority: Secretary of State; Assistant
Secretary of State; Deputy Secretary of State. *Indiana*
Office of Secretary of State
Statehouse
Suite 201
Indianapolis, IN 46204
317-232-6532
http://www.in.gov/sos/notary/seal.html **Fee: no charge**

Iowa Apostille - Authentication Offices
Designated Authority: Secretary of State; Deputy Secretary
of State *Iowa*
Office of Secretary of State
Lucas Building
First Floor, Public Service
Des Moines, IA 50319
515-281-5204
http://www.sos.state.ia.us

Fee: $5.00

Kansas Apostille - Authentication Offices
Designated Authority: Secretary of State; Deputy Secretary
of State *Kansas*
Office of Secretary of State
Memorial Hall, 1st Floor
Topeka, KS 66612-1594
785-296-4564
http://www.kssos.org

Fee: $7.50

Kentucky Apostille - Authentication Offices
Designated Authority: Secretary of State; Assistant
Secretary of State; any Deputy Assistant Secretary of State.
Kentucky
Office of Secretary of State
Capitol Building
P.O. Box 718
Frankfort, KY 40602-0178
502-564-7330
Fee: $5.00
http://www.kysos.com

Louisiana Apostille - Authentication Offices
Designated Authority: Secretary of State; Assistant
Secretary of State. *Louisiana*
Office of Secretary of State
P.O. Box 94125
Baton Rouge, LA 70804-9125
504-342-4981
Fee: $5.00
http://www.sec.state.la.us/comm/comm-index.htm

Maine Apostille - Authentication Offices
Designated Authority: Secretary of State. *Maine*
Office of Secretary of State
Bureau of Corporations
Elections and Commissions
101 State House Station
Augusta, ME 04333-0101
207-624-7650
http://www.state.me.us/sos/cec/rcn/notary/authapos.ht
m

Fee: $10.00

Maryland Apostille - Authentication Offices
Designated Authority: Secretary of State; Deputy Secretary
of State.

Maryland
Office of Secretary of State
Statehouse
Annapolis, MD 21401
410-974-5520
http://www.sos.state.md.us/sos/certif/html/certif2c.html
#apos **Fee: $5.00**

Massachusetts Apostille - Authentication Offices
Designated Authority: Secretary of State. *Massachusetts*
Secretary of the Commonwealth
Public Records Division
Commissions Section
McCormack Building, Room 1719
One Ashburton Place
Boston, MA 02108
617-727-2832
http://www.state.ma.us/sec/pre/precom/comidx.htm

Fee: $3.00

Michigan Apostille - Authentication Offices
Designated Authority: Department of State. *Michigan*
Department of State
Office of the Great Seal
7064 Crowner Boulevard
Lansing, MI 48918
517-373-2531
http://www.michigan.gov/sos/1,1607,7-127-1638_8734---
,00.html

Fee: $1.00

Minnesota Apostille - Authentication Offices
Designated Authority: Secretary of State; Deputy Secretary
of State. *Minnesota*
Secretary of State"s Office

180 State Office Bldg.
St. Paul, MN 55155
651-296-2803
http://www.sos.state.mn.us/uccd/authinfo.html

Fee: $5.00

Mississippi Apostille - Authentication Offices
Designated Authority: Secretary of State; Deputy Secretary
of State. *Mississippi*
Office of Secretary of State
P.O. Box 136
Jackson, MS 39205-0136
601-359-1615
http://www.sos.state.ms.us/busserv/notaries/notaries.ht
ml

Fee: $5.00

Missouri Apostille - Authentication Offices
Designated Authority: Secretary of State; any Assistant
Secretary of State. *Missouri*
Office of Secretary of State
Commission Division
600 West Main, Room 367
Jefferson City, MO 65102
573-751-2783
http://www.sos.mo.gov/business/commissions/certify.asp

Fee: $10.00

Montana Apostille - Authentication Offices
Designated Authority: Secretary of State; Deputy Secretary
of State. *Montana*
Office of the Secretary of State
Notary/Certification Division
State Capitol Rm 260
PO Box 202801

Helena MT 59620-2801
UPS-FedEx-DHL- etc. address: 1236 E 6th Ave Helena MT
59620
406-444-1877 (Tuesdays - Thursdays only)
http://sos.state.mt.us/css/Notary/Certifications.asp

email: sosnotary@state.mt.us This e-mail address is being
protected from spambots. You need JavaScript enabled to
view it
Fee: $10.00 per document

Nebraska Apostille - Authentication Offices
Designated Authority: Secretary of State; Any Deputy
Secretary of State *Nebraska*
Office of Secretary of State
Notary Division
Box 95104
State Capitol
Lincoln, NE 68509
402-471-2558
http://www.sos.state.ne.us/Notary/notauth.htm

Fee: $10.00

Nevada Apostille - Authentication Offices
Designated Authority: Secretary of State; Deputy Secretary
of State. *Nevada*
Secretary of State
101 N. Carson Street, #3
Carson City, NV 89701-4786
775-684-5708
http://sos.state.nv.us/notary/apostille.htm

Fee: $20.00

New Hampshire Apostille - Authentication Offices
Designated Authority: Secretary of State; Chief Deputy
Secretary of State; Deputy Secretary of State. *New
Hampshire*

Office of Secretary of State
Statehouse
Room 204
Concord, NH 03301
603-271-3242
http://www.state.nh.us/sos/certific.htm

Fee: $5.00

New Jersey Apostille - Authentication Offices
Designated Authority: Secretary of State; Deputy Secretary of State *New Jersey*
Department of State
Notary Public Unit
Division of Commercial Recording
PO Box 452
Trenton, NJ 08625
609-530-6421
http://www.state.nj.us/treasury/revenue/dcr/programs/apostilles.htm

Fee: Regular Service: $25.00 Expedited Service: $35.00
Designated Authority: NJ Department of the Treasury, Division of Revenue

New Mexico Apostille - Authentication Offices
Designated Authority: Secretary of State - *New Mexico*
Office of the Secretary of State
State Capitol North Annex, Suite 300
Santa Fe, NM 87503
505-827-3600
http://www.sos.state.nm.us/notary-cert.htm

Fee: $3.00

New York Apostille - Authentication Offices
Designated Authority: Secretary of State *New York*
Upstate Counties

Miscellaneous Records
One Commerce Plaza
99 Washington Avenue, Suite 600.
Albany, NY 12231
518-474-4770
http://www.dos.state.ny.us

Fee: $10.00
Designated Authority: Secretary of State; Executive Deputy
Secretary of State; any Deputy Secretary of State; any
Special Deputy Secretary of State.

Down State Counties
New York authorities in Albany advise that documents
issued in the nine down state counties are authenticated
under the Convention by the New York City office. The
nine down state counties are New York, Kings, Queens,
Bronx, Westchester, Nassau, Suffolk, Rockland and
Richmond. The address of the New York Department of
State, Certification Unit is 123 William Street, New York,
New York 10038-3804, tel: (212) 417-5800. **Fee: $10.00**

North Carolina Apostille - Authentication Offices
Designated Authority: Secretary of State - *North
Carolina*
Office of Secretary of State
Authentication Division
PO Box 29622
Raleigh, NC 27626-0622
919-807-2140
http://www.secretary.state.nc.us/authen

Fee: $10.00

North Dakota Apostille - Authentication Offices
Designated Authority: Secretary of State; Deputy Secretary
of State *North Dakota*
Office of Secretary of State

Capitol Building
600 E Boulevard Ave., Dept 108

Bismarck, ND 58505
701-328-2900
http://www.state.nd.us/sec

Fee: $10.00

Ohio Apostille - Authentication Offices
Designated Authority: Secretary of State; Deputy Secretary
of State. *Ohio*
Office of the Secretary of State
30 East Broad St.
15th Fl.
Columbus, OH 43266-0418
877-767-6446
http://www.sos.state.oh.us/SOS/Text.aspx?page=1150&As
pxAutoDetectCookieSupport=1**Fee: $5.00**

Oklahoma Apostille - Authentication Offices
Designated Authority: Secretary of State; Assistant
Secretary of State. *Oklahoma*
Office of Secretary of State
2300 N. Lincoln
Room 101
Oklahoma City, OK 73105
405-521-4211
http://www.sos.state.ok.us

Fee: $25.00 (cashiers check or money order)

Oregon Apostille - Authentication Offices
Designated Authority: Secretary of State; Assistant
Secretary of State; Budget Officer of the Secretary of State.
Oregon
Office of Secretary of State
255 Capitol St. Suite 151, Salem OR 97310

503-986-2200.
http://www.filinginoregon.com/notary/index.htm

Fee: $10.00

Pennsylvania Apostille - Authentication Offices
Designated Authority: Secretary of State; Deputy Secretary
of State; Acting Secretary of State; Assistant to the
Secretary of State. *Pennsylvania*
Department of State
Bureau of Commissions
Elections and Legislation
North Office Building
Room 210
Harrisburg, PA 17120
717-787-5280
http://www.dos.state.pa.us/bcel/certifications/certificatio
ns.html

Fee: $15.00

Rhode Island Apostille - Authentication Offices
Designated Authority: Secretary of the Commonwealth;
Executive Deputy Secretary of the Commonwealth.

Rhode Island
Office of Secretary of State Authentication/Certifications
148 W, River Street.
Providence, RI 02904
401-222-1487
http://www.sec.state.ri.us/corps/apostille/authen.html

Fee: $5.00

South Carolina Apostille - Authentication Offices
Designated Authority: Secretary of State; First Deputy
Secretary of State; Deputy Secretary of State *South
Carolina*

Office of Secretary of State
P.O. Box 11350

Columbia, SC 29211
803-734-2119
http://www.scsos.com/notariesbc.htm

Fee: $2.00

South Dakota Apostille - Authentication Offices
Designated Authority: Secretary of State *South Dakota*
Office of Secretary of State
500 East Capitol
Pierre, SD 57501-5077
605-773-5004
http://www.state.sd.us/sos/Notaries/apostilles_and_auth
entications.htm

Fee: $2.00

Tennessee Apostille - Authentication Offices
Designated Authority: Secretary of State; Deputy Secretary
of State *Tennessee*
Office of Secretary of State
James K. Polk Building
Division of Business Services
312 Eighth Avenue North
6th Floor, William R. Snodgrass Tower
Nashville, TN 37243
615-741-3699
http://www.state.tn.us/sos/bus_svc/apostilles.htm

Fee: $2.00

Texas Apostille - Authentication Offices
Designated Authority: Secretary of State. *Texas*
Office of Secretary of State
P.O. Box 12079
Austin, TX 78711

512-463-5705
http://www.sos.state.tx.us/authinfo.shtml

Fee: $10.00

Utah Apostille - Authentication Offices
Designated Authority: Secretary of State; Assistant
Secretary of State *Utah*
Office of the Lieutenant Governor
210 State Capitol
Salt Lake City, UT 84145-8414
801-538-1040
http://governor.state.ut.us/lt_gover/internationaltemplat
e.html

**Fee: Certifying Notary"s Seal: $10.00 Apostille:
$5.00**
Designated Authority: Lieutenant Governor; Deputy
Lieutenant Governor; Administrative

Vermont Apostille - Authentication Offices
Designated Authority: Secretary of State - *Vermont*
Office of Secretary of State
109 State St.
Montpelier, VT 05609-1103
802-828-2308
http://www.sec.state.vt.us

Fee: $2.00

Virginia Apostille - Authentication Offices
Designated Authority: Secretary of the Commonwealth:
Attn: Authentication Department *Virginia*
Office of Secretary of Commonwealth
Attn: Authentication Department
1111 East Broad Street, 4th Floor
Richmond, VA 23219
804-786-2441
http://www.soc.state.va.us

Fee: $10.00

Washington Apostille - Authentication Offices
Designated Authority: Secretary of the Commonwealth; Chief Clerk, Office of the Secretary of Commonwealth.
Washington
Office of the Secretary of State
Corporations Division
Apostille and Certificate Program
PO Box 40228
Olympia, WA 98504-0228
360-586-2268
http://www.secstate.wa.gov/apostilles

Fee: $15.00

Designated Authority: Secretary of State; Assistant Secretary of State; Director, Department of Licensing.

West Virginia Apostille - Authentication Offices
Designated Authority: Secretary of State - *West Virginia*
Office of Secretary of State
Capitol Building
1900 Kanawha Blvd. East
No. 157-K
Charleston, WV 25305-0770
304-558-6000
http://www.wvsos.com/execrecords/other/authentication.htm

Fee: $10.00

Wisconsin Apostille - Authentication Offices
Designated Authority: Secretary of State; Under Secretary of State; any Deputy Secretary of State. *Wisconsin*
Office of Secretary of State
P.O. Box 7848
Madison, WI 53707-7848

608-266-3159
http://badger.state.wi.us/agencies/sos/authen.htm

Fee: $10.00

Wyoming Apostille - Authentication Offices
Designated Authority: Secretary of State; Assistant Secretary of State. *Wyoming*
Office of Secretary of State
The Capitol
Cheyenne, WY 82002-0020
307-777-5342
http://soswy.state.wy.us/authenti/authenti.htm

Fee: $3.00

American Samoa Apostille - Authentication Offices
Designated Authority: Secretary of State; Deputy Secretary of State. *American Samoa*
Office of the Governor
Pago Pago, AS 96799
011-684-633-4116
http://www.amsamoa.com

Designated Authority: Secretary of American Samoa; Attorney General of American Samoa.

Guam Apostille - Authentication Offices
Designated Authority: Office of the Governor *Guam (Territory of)*
Office of the Governor
P.O. Box 2950
Agana, GU 96910
011-671-472-1537
http://www.admin.gov.gu/doa

Northern Mariana Islands Apostille - Authentication Offices
Designated Authority: Department of Administration

Northern Mariana Islands (Commonwealth of the)
Designated Authority: Attorney General; Acting Attorney General; Clerk of theCourt, Commonwealth Trial Court; Deputy Clerk, Commonwealth Trial Court
http://www.saipan.com/gov
Supreme Court of Puerto Rico
Office of Notarial Inspection
P.O. Box 190860
San Juan, PR 00919-0860
787-763-8816
http://www.lexjuris.com/lexnotaria.htm

U.S. Virgin Islands Apostille - Authentication
OfficesDesignated Authority: Supreme Court of Puerto Rico U.S. Virgin Islands

Office of the Lieutenant Governor7 & 8 King St.Christiansted, St. Croix, USVI 00802

340-774-2991

http://www.ltg.gov.vi/Departments/Administration/index.html

That's it for the where to obtain an apostille. Back in the day, there was no such thing as an apostille for working in Korea. But thanks to a fanatic Korean organization with a racist agenda, who are quick to prosecute and persecute any foreigner wrong-doings, particularly Western teachers, an apostille was approved.

Thus, as of Fall 2010, the Korean government changed its policies for NSETs. All U.S. citizens must obtain an *apostilled* FBI criminal background check directly from FBI Headquarters.

The Apostille – Notarization – Certification – FBI Check

-Yes, indeed, the times they are a changin'

Obtaining an FBI Criminal Background Check

Don't have it, don't need it; but you will, so let's get started.

The FBI CBC (Criminal Background Check) can take anywhere from one to three months to obtain, so it's wise to begin ASAP. Beware, however, that your apostille docs are valid for only six months after the apostille date. They must be valid when you enter Korea, so you should be sure that you're going to find a job within six months. If not, your apostile docs will expire and you'll have to begin the process again.

1. Download and fill out the *FBI application form* at -

https://forms.fbi.gov/departmental-order-website-questionnaire

2. You can obtain your fingerprints at any authorized company or the police station. If you are in Korea, simply go to your local police station and get them done on a fingerprint card issued by the police station or download the *FBI fingerprint card* at –

http://www.fbi.gov/about-us/cjis/background-checks/standard-fingerprint-form-fd-258

Print it and take it with you.

3. Attach your application with your fingerprint card and $18 money order, cashier's check, or via credit card information (no personal or business checks are accepted) an download the following:

http://www.fbi.gov/about-us/cjis/background-checks/credit-card-payment-form

Remember to check the *checklist* to ensure that you've included everything:

http://www.fbi.gov/about-us/cjis/background-checks/fbi-identification-record-request-checklist

For instructions on submitting an *Identification Record Request* to the FBI-
http://www.fbi.gov/about-us/cjis/background-checks/submitting-an-identification-record-request-to-the-fbi

4. Make sure to also include a separate note stating:
"Please provide an FBI seal and signature from a Division Officer for the purpose of obtaining a Federal aostille."
     The FBI seal and signature are *required* in order to get an apostille. They must be requested specifically and can simply be written on a piece of paper and included in the application.

5. Mail to:

FBI CJIS Division – Record Request
1000 Custer Hollow Road
Clarksburg, WV 26306.

If a follow up is needed regarding the status of your application, call the FBI office in West Virginia. If you need to follow up about the status of your application, call **304-625-5590**.

6. Once you receive the CBC, proceed to step 2: obtaining an apostille.

Obtaining an Apostille for a FBI Criminal Background Check:

1. Download the Authentication form (aka cover letter) from –

http://www.state.gov/documents/organization/63001.pdf

Website info: http://www.state.gov/m/a/auth/

2. **Fees:**
Expect to pay $8.00 per document.
A personal/company check or money order are acceptable and must be made payable to: *U.S. Department of State.*
Visa, MasterCard, Discover, and American Express are accepted for *walk-in service* only.

3. Mail in documents.

Include your form (cover letter), check for $8.00, your processed CBC and a SASE.

Documents received without a return envelope and postage will be returned through the State Department regular mail, which may take two-three weeks longer. You may use Fed/Ex, UPS, and express mail services for faster receipt and return of your documents. However, you must enclose a prepaid air bill and envelope.

Mail to:

U.S. Department of State
Authentications Office
518 23rd Street NW.
SA-1
Washington, DC 20520.

How to get an apostille for your degree

Before even thinking about an apostille, you'll first want to have your degree notarized. Be aware that you must have it notarized in the same state where you will obtain the apostille.

As confusing as it may be, you are not required to get your degree notarized and apostilled in the state where you obtained your degree. You are free to do it in any state you want. Just keep in mind that before you obtain an apostille that you must first have your degree notarized as stated above.

Public Notary

You can find a notary at many places – post offices, banks, car dealerships, and many others. One point you'll want to watch out for is that you don't want the notary to notarize your original diploma. Rather, ask him/her to notarize a photocopy of your diploma (be sure to bring the original with you). As an added precaution, you may want to call the notary and ask what is required by way of documents. I've heard that some had to bring their transcripts with them. Before you leave the notary, make sure that they have completed the following:

- Your name and signature
- The notary's name and signature
- The notary's seal
- The date the notary's license expires
- The date you had it notarized
- The county and state where the notary is licensed

All of the above can be written on the back of the photocopy of the diploma.

Upon completion, mail your diploma to the Secretary of State to obtain the apostille. Once again, you'll want to get the apostille in the same state where you obtained the notarization.

There is usually a fee, so you'll want to contact the secretary of state in your state and find out what the fee is as well as what kinds of payment they accept. You will also want to include a cover letter which should include the following:

(Your State) Secretary of State
Authentication Department
(Apostille request)
Date: _____
Name: _____
My phone: _____
My email: _____
Country where documents will be sent: _____
Please return documents via enclosed, postage-paid
envelope
Signature: _____

Next let's have a look at a few examples of an apostille. The first is from the USA – formats differ a bit from state to state, and an apostille from the UK. These are followed by a sample of an E2 Health Statement necessary for an E2 teaching visa, and, finally, the visa application form.

Apostille

(Convention de La Haye du 5 Octobre 1961)

1. Country: **United States of America**

    This public document

2. has been signed by **Nancy T. Sunshine**

3. acting in the capacity of **County Clerk**

4. bears the seal/stamp of the county of **Kings**

Certified

5. At New York, New York   6. the 25th day of June 2009

7. by Special Deputy Secretary of State, State of New York

8. No. NYC-10686541A

9. Seal/Stamp   10. Signature

James Bizzarri
Special Deputy Secretary of State

APOSTILLE

(Hague Convention of 5 October 1961 / Convention de La Haye du 5 octobre 1961)

UNITED KINGDOM OF GREAT BRITAIN AND NORTHERN IRELAND

1. Country: United Kingdom of Great Britain and Northern Ireland
Pays: Royaume-Uni de Grande-Bretagne et d'Irlande du Nord

This public document / Le présent acte public

2. Has been signed by   **Ashley Davis**
a été signé par

3. Acting in the capacity of   **Officer of the Companies Registration Office, Cardiff.**
agissant en qualité de

4. Bears the seal/stamp of
est revêtu du sceau/timbre de

Certified/Attesté

5. at London/à Londres   6. the/le   **30 March 2010**

7. by Her Majesty's Principal Secretary of State for Foreign and Commonwealth Affairs /
par le Secrétaire d'Etat Principal de Sa Majesté aux Affaires Etrangères et du Commonwealth.

8. Number/sous No   **I458166**

9. Stamp: 10. Signature   **D. O'Sullivan**
timbre:

For the Secretary of State / Pour le Secrétaire d'Etat

If this document is to be used in a country which is not party to the Hague Convention of 5th October 1961, it should be presented to the consular section of the mission representing that country.

An apostille or legalisation certificate only confirms that the signature, seal or stamp on the document is genuine. It does not mean that the content of the document is correct or that the Foreign & Commonwealth Office approves of the content

E-2 Health Statement

출입국·외국인정책본부
KOREA IMMIGRATION SERVICE

> **E-2 Applicant's Health Statement**

This form is to check the E-2 Visa Applicant's Health. Please fill in the blanks accurately and truthfully. Please keep in mind that if you fill in the blanks with incorrect information, you

would face disadvantages such as visa disapproval, cancellation of stay permit, deportation,

etc.

1) NAME IN FULL(As in Passport)	2) DATE OF BIRTH	
3) NATIONALITY	4) SEX	5) PASSPORT NUMBER

6) Have you ever caught infectious diseases that threaten Public Health before?

Yes □ (Infectious Disease name:), No □

7) Have you ever taken any Narcotic (Drug) OR Have you ever been addicted to alcohol? Yes □ (Narcotic name:), No □
8) Have you ever received treatment for Mental/ Neurotic/ Emotional Disorder? Yes □ (Disorder name:), No □
9) Are OR were you HIV (AIDS) positive? Yes □ , No □
10) Have you had any serious Diseases OR Injuries for the last 5 years? Yes □ (name & recent situation:), No □

NOTICE:

You MUST make Alien Registration at your District Immigration Office (OR Branch Office) within 90 days after your arrival in Korea. And, when you register, You MUST submit your Health Certificate obtained from the hospital which has been designated by the Korean Government.

Date: _____

Applicant's Signature: _____

[별첨 7][별지 제 17 호 서식]

APPLICATION FOR VISA

(Author's note: I have removed the Chinese and Korean characters for sake of clarity)

PHOTO

35 × 45 ㎜

1. Surname

2. Given Names

3. Date of Birth

    Y   **M**   **D**

4. Sex

    □ **M**   □ **F**

5. Nationality

6. Place of Birth

7. Passport Number

8. Classification

   DP OF OR

9. Date of Issue

10. Place of Issue

11. Issuing Authority

12. **Expiry Date**

13. **Marital Status**

   ☐ **married**   ☐ **single**

14. **Spouse's Name**

15. **Spouse's Nationality**

16. **Occupation**

17. **Name and Address of Present Employer**

18. **Business Phone Number**

19. **Purpose of Entry(explain fully)**

20. **Probable Date of Entry**

21. **Desired Length of Stay**

22. **Home Address**   **Phone No.**

23. **Address in Korea**   **Phone No.**

24. **Previous Visit (If Any)**

25. **Have You Ever Been Issued a Korean Visa?**   ☐
Yes   ☐ **No**

When?   **Where?**   **What Type of Visa**

26. **Have You Ever Been Refused a Korean Visa?**

☐ **Yes**   ☐**No**

When?   Where?

What Type of Visa?

27. Who Will Pay For Your Trip?

28. Has Your Korean Visa Ever Been Cancelled or
Revoked?

☐ Yes   ☐ No

29. Countries Where You Have Lived or Traveled
During The Past 5 Years

30. Accompanying Family

Nationality

Name

Sex

Date of Birth

31. Guarantor or Reference in Korea

Name

Address

Phone No.

Relationship

I declare that the statements made in this application are true and correct to the best of my knowledge and belief, that I will observe the provisions of the Immigration Law of the Republic of Korea and that I will not engage in any activities irrelevant to the purpose of entry stated herein. Besides, I am fully aware that any false or misleading statement may result in the refusal of a visa, and that possession of a visa does not entitle the **bearer to enter** the Republic of Korea upon arrival at the port of entry if he/she is found inadmissible.

日 DATE OF APPLICATION

SIGNATURE OF APPLICANT

FOR OFFICIAL USE ONLY

Chapter 13

Choosing a Venue

—Wherever you go, there you are.

Confused? If you aren't than something is amiss with this missive. I can hear the gears grinding in the old clunker: *"Where should I begin? Where should I teach? What is the best choice?"* These are all valid questions, of course. Choosing a venue is a Herculean effort; that much is obvious. Just so, I'll try to make things a bit more humane for you, so you can maintain your current level of sanity (?)

I've grouped the government sponsored programs together because of their similarities. They'll be compared to hagwons. Universities and colleges are not included because if you don't have a graduate degree, forget it. Be aware that some of these points have pro as well as con aspects.

Hagwons

Pro:

None—but I jest!?

1. Less populated classes. The most I've ever taught was 14, which is far too populated for a 50 minute class. Said class

was an adult free-speaking class, by the way. You should be aware that it's perfectly possible to have 14 children in a class, which makes me shutter. The more popular a hagwon is, the more students it has, so think about that if you choose a hagwon. Ask the director or current NSET about the average student population in each class.

2. Sleep! Well...sometimes. Again, check with the director or current NSET and have him/her guarantee no morning classes. Some hagwons may have morning adult classes or kindergarten classes, so you can effectively forget having a beer or ten after work.

3. No KET. No KET means less politics in or out of class. You're on your own and it's *you* who make it or break it. In small classes, this is a blessing. In large classes where classroom management issues arise, you may find yourself pleading for a KET-like situation. It also frees up your time because you don't have to prepare materials with the KET.

4. No bureaucracy. You have only the director to deal with, and sometimes the head-teacher, so less politics (I loathe politics) However, as you have seen, directors can sometimes be the armpit of what is an otherwise decent venue. They may or may not back you up if you have discipline problems with students, or may cheat you of your wage, cut your vacation time, and other unpleasantries.

5. You'll be working with other NSETs. In big franchise hagwons there are sometimes ten or more NSETS, so you'll not be lonely.

6. Directors usually won't require you to desk-warm for an unreasonable amount of time, if at all.

Con:

1. Less pay. Thirty hours of contact time per week for a rather miserly wage. Ouch! This wage hasn't changed in many years.

2. Less benefits. Very few hagwons offer a contract renewal bonus, or added days of vacation upon renewing. Add to that, not many offer round-trip airfare, either.

3. Stress. Stress in many forms, that is. Hagwons outside of Gyeongi province typically do not charge parents much, so you'll be under great pressure to perform and to perform well. We're talking 50 percent teaching and the remainder divided between entertainment, both personal and otherwise. Therefore, student retention is of utmost importance.

4. Preset curricula. If you're new to teaching, this could actually be a pro. If you have experience, than you're not going to like this one much. I've discussed this earlier in the book.

5. No preschoolers. Again, this one can go either way. If you love the little ones and don't mind saliva, urine, diapers, and breast grabbing, this one is pro. If not, you know the reasons why. Add to that, many hagwons have at least one preschool class. Do your research.

6. Much less vacation time. Typically, hagwon vacation time is 10 days or less. Worse yet, you won't have a choice as to when you are able to take your vacation.

7. Classes can sometimes run very late.

8. Your director may stress you out if parents are dissatisfied with their children's progress.

Government Programs

Pro:

1. They are government funded programs, so there is less contract nonsense. However, be aware that contractual obligations are sometimes not compatible with all schools. Certain schools have enough leverage to void certain points of the contract, such as contact hours. Complaints normally fall on deaf ears.

2. Less contact time. Most schools require 22 hours contact time per week, but you may well find yourself teaching over 22 hours, despite what your contract states. However, contact time over 22 hours is considered overtime, for which you'll be compensated.

3. Longer vacation. Normally, government programs allow teachers 18 days vacation; eight in summer and ten in winter. Some schools will negotiate with you regarding when to take your vacation days.

4. 11 days paid sick leave.

5. Contract renewal bonus. This includes a wage increase and vacation increase.

6. Travel allowance should you be farmed out to other schools.

7. Korean co-teachers. Can sometimes be a blessing, sometimes a curse. I know many public school teachers

who cringe when they think of their KETS. Just so, there are just as many that couldn't live without a KET in the classroom. It's really a crap shoot.

8. No director. Just so, you'll have a hell of a lot more bureaucracy to deal with.

9. Much less lesson planning. Typically, you'll write three to seven lesson plans per week.

10. No monthly student assessments.

11. Program improvement. Despite what many teachers say, the government program officials do listen to NSET complaints. These complaints are what motivate improvement, however gradual it may be.

Con

1. Early morning start. No problem here if you're a morning person. If you aren't, you're in for a treat.

2. Desk warming. You will have downtime in which you must stay at school, so get used to it.

3. Unexpected schedule changes. This happens to every teacher at every school; if you can roll with it, no problem.

4. Large classes. Depending on your school, you'll have 25 to 40 students per class, and you'll only see those students once or twice a week.

5. Classroom management. If you're unfortunate to have an uncooperative KET, you're going to have deal with

student management issues, which can stress you to no end.

6. Summer camps. Great, you get to spend your vacation designing and teaching summer camp.

7. Poorly written text books. Unauthentic language usage and incredibly boring texts.

Kindergarten

I know I haven't exactly painted a rosy picture of kindergartens, but I feel I've not been entirely fair about the matter.

Pro:

1. Recall 'tabula rasa'? Empty slate, folks, that, in a nutshell, describes preschoolers. Teaching preschool can be extraordinarily rewarding. You will be responsible for what is perhaps their introduction to English. Add to that the fact that you'll have evidence of weekly progress.

2. My sons were once preschoolers, so I know well how affectionate they can be; not only to me, but to their teachers, also. If you have notions of having children of your own in the future, teaching preschoolers will aid you greatly once you do.

Con

I've already discussed what occurs in the kindergartens, so no further discussion is necessary.

Part Three

TEACHING CHILDREN

Chapter 14

Tips and Techniques

The challenge of teaching children

> *"There's no use trying," Alice said, "One can't believe impossible things."*

—Lewis Carroll, Through the Looking Glass

re Korean children really that different than children in the West? The answer, naturally, is yes and no. They have in common what children everywhere have in common: they seek fun. But the similarity tends to end there. Really, Korean children, as mentioned many times throughout this book, have very little by way of childhood. This does not make for happy children, positively motivated children, or well-adjusted children, and it carries over into adulthood – baggage, baggage; thus, the challenge in the classroom. I don't care which venue you find yourself teaching at, the challenge you face when teaching Korean children can be overwhelming at times. You'll find your 120 or less hours of ESL/EFL certificate instruction did not prepare you for what is to come.

I came to Korea, fresh out of university, and idealistic as hell. Yes, I am going to make a difference. My first week in a kid's class changed all of that.

Carol Read, a teacher whom I greatly admire, stated that, ideally, we want to teach kids to learn successfully and to have them become passionate, considerate people. We want them to become responsible, self-aware, and reflective learners. They aren't our kids, so we have no idea what they want or need to learn in the future, but we do know that we want to equip them to become competent and confident speakers of English. Dream on, Carol. To a certain extent, that is.

Korean kindergarten and early elementary school children still have a childhood, so the above is actually doable; however, after fourth grade things tend to devolve for the children. They become more uncooperative, unmotivated and teachable moments become few and far between.

It took me a hell of a lot of time, research, and experience to discover these techniques, so pay attention, class! And keep in mind that these techniques are most pragmatic in the hagwon. Kudos go out to Carol for her brilliant ideas; many of which I've used successfully.

NLP and Kinesthetic Learning

If you're not familiar with it, NLP simply means Neuro Linguistic Programming. I'm not going to waste time describing NLP because the information exists on the internet. Much of NLP is new-age nonsense, but if you really try to wade through the rubbish, a few key NLP concepts become quite helpful in the classroom via such techniques as pacing, leading, rapport, setting examples etc., that we should be using as a matter of course and which were being used long before someone gave it a name and profited from it. If you've ever heard of Tony Robbins, you've heard of NLP.

In the NLP realm, the following sentence is repeatedly used: *"Pretend it works, try it, and notice the results you get. If you don't get the result you want, try something else.*" It's just common sense, really.

An example of this could be the following scenario which, for all intents and purposes, happens in every class you teach. If you keep close watch on how students react to a given activity, you'll come to know whether they are bored to tears, or, conversely, excited by the activity via the non-verbal clues students communicate to us throughout the class. If you find a negative reaction to your activity, simply adjust your lesson plan to prevent negative outcomes, or simply give them a breather to clear the air or bring them back to planet earth.

An example, pragmatically speaking, is when you march on to class and oddly (?) find that students have some get up and go. They are jumping around, having that rarity known as fun and are not ready to focus. Ordinarily, you walk into this kind of classroom and think to yourself, *"Another hagwon hell day."* And it usually is.

It's obvious that the students are giving you all kinds of visual cues. The last thing you want to do is to fight those cues. Using NLP, you'll want to use what is aptly named *"pacing,"* which is simply rolling with the cues the students are giving you. Say, for example, you were going to begin the day's lesson using the text, which ordinarily bores the students to death. Rather than fight all those cues by yelling and getting angry, which are counterproductive, go with them by beginning the class with some kind of short activity that will harness all of that pent-up energy. Doing so will usually lead them to calm down. I've used a lot of Simon Says when I used to teach children in a high energy classroom, provided they are familiar with the vocabulary.

Conversely, if you walk into a classroom of exhausted, uncooperative children, than do the opposite. Rather than use an aerobic activity, I would use a low-key activity that did not require much focus or energy. For example, I've taught vocabulary using Kinesthetic Learning (yet more jargon) which, despite it's rather complex name, does have educational value; it helps children to make connections between language and concepts. So, for example, I'll lay my head down on the table and say "*Let's sleep.*" While my head is down, I'll make snoring sounds and say "*Let's snore.*" After which I'll roll my head around on the table and say "*Let's dream.*" I'll then get up, eyes closed, and walk around the table with my arms extended zombie-like and say "*Let's sleep walk.*" The kids usually cooperate and have fun, and when all is said and done, they usually become more cooperative and awake.

They call it NLP and Kinesthetic learning, I call it humanist teaching. Point is, I'm tuning into my students wave length (NLP), which makes it easier for me to empathize with my students. Much of the time, it makes the class less of a nightmare and more of an enjoyable experience for all.

Being flexible while teaching kids is imperative. But how do you include flexibility during the normal course of your class? We can be flexible in the way we:

- **ask and answer questions** – what kind of questions we use: tag, open/closed? Who asks and answers questions?
- **choose topics** – topic choice can be decided by trying to discover the kid's interests and putting those interests to work.

- **use activities** – what do you want the kids to do? Stand up, stay seated, move around?
- **organize the class** – you can organize the kids according to anything you wish. For example, by ability, gender, friendship.
- **recycle activities** – if the kids enjoy a particular activity more than any other and want to do it again.
- **correct errors or give feedback** – orally, written, to the class or individually.
- **time your activities/lessons** – new activities or lessons sometime take longer than we would like, or they are too difficult for the kids.

Again, I can't stress enough the significance of flexibility in children's classes. My suggestions are all based on experience, with the help of Carol Read's input, so they are extremely valid. If you're flexible, your children's classes will not bring you so much stress, frustration, and disappointment. If you find that conflict is unavoidable, try to remain calm. Speak in a low, slow voice, and don't go into a K-rage. You don't want to be one of many who post hagwon horror stories on a blog, and your students will have no idea what in hell you're yelling about. You may seem highly comical to them, so just forget venting.

I have discussed children's energy levels earlier in the book, but I would also like to say a little more on energy management.

- Be flexible. If you walk into your kid's class and find that chaos reigns, don't fight it, roll with it. Conversely, if you find the children getting restless during class, take a break and do a physical activity, of which there are many.

- Whether you teach songs, rhymes, chants or stories, teach physical actions to accompany them. This can be extremely difficult for the macho types, but get over your insecurity; the kids really enjoy it and they learn to associate movement with meaning. It also gives them the opportunity to get up and move around.

- Use physical movement for other activities, also. If, for example, you have sentences, phrases, clauses, or pictures on the walls of the classroom, you can have the kids get up and read or point them out as you give them cues or prompts. Again, it gives them a break.

- Have them work together on various projects. This will teach them cooperation and how to work in a non-threatening and non-competitive way.

- If you're teaching the little ones (ages three to six), remember that having them sit down for long periods of time, say ten minutes, is an eternity to them.

- Don't be overzealous, like I once was, about correct pronunciation. Don't forget that you, too, were once language learners and that pronunciation was secondary to communication. Correcting pronunciation halts the flow of the lesson and is counterproductive in nearly every way. Save correction for high school and university students, but only when teaching them in a hagwon or as a private tutor.

I would like to end this unit with a joke...or, if you've been here for a long time, a truism that Koreans tell about one another:

A Korean is visiting America where he gets hit by a car and is lying badly injured on the road. The car driver gets out, runs over to him and asks, "How are you?"
The Korean replies, "Fine, thank you. And you?"

Part Four

WHAT TO KNOW BEFORE COMING TO KOREA

Chapter 15

Exams and Systematic Child Abuse

(1) States Parties recognize the right of the child to rest and leisure, to engage in play and recreational activities appropriate to the age of the child and to participate freely in cultural life and the arts.

– Article 31, Clause 1 – Declaration of the Rights of the Child
– United Nations

Comprehending the Exam System in Korea

The following is based on teaching Middle school students. I've been told by Korean teachers that about 60 percent of the students' final grade is based on written exam results. The usual exam routine is as follows: during the first semester, students take their mid-term followed by their final exams. The second semester follows the same routine. Thus, a total of four multiple-choice exams which are filled in on OMR cards and marked electronically. These four exams will decide the students' score.

Naturally, the issue here is the exam type: multiple-choice. How in hell anyone can use this type of exam, other than downright laziness, for midterm and final tests is beyond this teacher.

NSETs bring this up with their KETs at teacher get-togethers, but it always falls on deaf ears. Why change what works, KETs reply.

Sadly, teachers will find it impossible to change the testing status quo, so I suggest you do what I mentioned in the section on texts: make the best of it. You can still make a difference on the outcome of their scores, even with the multiple choice format.

Now that I have children of my own attending middle and elementary school, I find myself understanding the system better. My ex-wife is also a teacher, so, naturally, she wants our sons to excel at these damned tests. It should be noted that many students really do care about their exam scores, but my sons are not among them. They make an effort for the sake of their mother, but they don't much care what happens in the classroom, for better or worse. So, more often than not, it's the *parents* who really care about the scores. And that, friends, is what I was explaining in the section on hagwons. Hagwons, recall, are not so much for conversation skills as they are for improving exam scores. You may also recall my rant on English as a school subject rather than a means of communication

I've spoken with – and taught, a number of native middle/elementary school teachers, and they experience the same conundrum. Most of the time, native teachers are in the classroom to simply help students with conversation, which is *not* on the exams. For that reason, the students really don't view the native teacher's classes as important. The students often want to relax and have fun, which means some sort of game, usually; or they simply catch up on their sleep.

You can either roll with it or go against it. I advise you to go against it. I don't know about you, but I've always had a need to feel like I was teaching for reasons other than entertainment. And, so, you, too, should be determined to have greater input into what is being taught in the classroom. As soon as the new semester begins, much to the students' dismay, you should begin teaching material from their English textbooks, and write exam questions based on that material. Next, proofread the English exam papers while they are in the preparation phase and, finally, prepare the best review lessons as possible that will allow students to achieve high scores on the exam. Does it work? You bet it does.

More on Exams

Despite the popularity of English in the job market, there are, as of this writing, no standardized tests in the school system to determine English language proficiency. This is also true, to a lesser degree, at the university level where students are not accessed on their writing and speaking skills. The focus is on test taking, naturally.

The test that is used is the Junior Test of the English Language for International Communication (TOEIC). The TOEIC, whether junior or not, is big business. It is a test of language proficiency that is used to establish a set of standards for job place reading, writing and listening. These days, they have also included assessment in speaking skills.

Koreans bemoan this test, and I've come to hate the damn thing, too. TOEIC is big money, folks. Many Koreans take the test five or six times, or until they have the score that they seek, which is expensive and places a burden on their finances. I wish that TOEIC would cease to exist, and it would if anyone had any sense at all. I believe, to a point, that my wish is coming true; many Korean institutions are beginning to use the OPIc as a means of assessment.

The CSAT is the much disliked college entrance exam. Do well, and you're on your way. Do poorly, and you'll find yourself in the rice paddies. The CSAT and TOEIC test scores are used by most companies to access job candidate's English skills. Focus for the HR people in these companies is on proficiency in writing and speaking.

As a former university professor, I've come to know that a large percentage of undergraduates lack English proficiency, particularly speaking. Well, it's become understandable after all these years in the system; the Korean English language curriculum is focused on one purpose, which is to ready the students to excel on the English Comprehension section of the CSAT.

Like the middle school exams, the test is a multiple-choice exam; again, very moronic. The importance of speaking and writing in class is minimized. The ultimate goal is, like the middle school tests, to achieve the highest score possible.

The results from *one* test with a very well-known format - hagown TOEIC teachers thrive on this format - is not a valid way of assessing language abilities. When taking a high-stakes test such as the CSAT, real learning and teaching are thrown out the door, for the most part. The test score, again, is all that is important. Sadly, important pragmatic elements of the language such as context, and cultural differences, are not salient.

I can't recall (must be getting old) where I read it, but I recall that Korea is behind Nepal in English proficiency based on the results of the IELTS, the International English Language Testing System. The test results state that Korean students fail to do well in speaking and writing. This is very true of my students, both past and present, at the university where I occasionally teach.

The only real cure here is to begin teaching the above skills at an early age. Also, the Korean government needs to better train KETs at primary and secondary schools, which I'm seeing with my ex-wife. She has taken numerous trips abroad sponsored by the Korean government to make her a more effective teacher of English. Better trained teachers would perhaps reduce the number of students that go overseas to study English.

A Further Critique of the Korean Educational System

Because I watch the job boards and read extensively, both for myself and my readers, I am privy to an abundance of information regarding English study in Korea. I think it is important that readers become aware of the *"why"* and *"how"* of not only English language instruction, but of the educational system in general. Thus armed, readers will come to understand just what drives and motivates Koreans, particularly Korean mothers, and perhaps allow you to become more aware of how the system works. I've discussed this a bit in the beginning of the book, but for the sake of clarity, let's have closer look at it.

Let's begin with English.

That Koreans invest enormous amounts of time, energy, and money learning English has already been discussed, as stated. However, the whole issue of English language study seems to be nothing but a divestiture; the

ROI continues to be very poor. By global standards, Korean learners are simply not improving.

To wit, speaking proficiency remains at the bottom. TOFEL test takers ranked 136th out of 161 nations in speaking skills. Not so good, right? But stay with me, there's more. They also scored an average 18 out of 30 speaking points on the Internet-based test (iBT), lower than the world average of 19.3 points. This information was provided by the Educational Testing Service3 (ETS), who administered the test, so it's quite reliable.

Koreans' overall TOEFL score was a dismal 78 out of 120, lower than the world average of 79. That score landed them 89th. The next year, they scored 77.

As for the other TOEFL skills, listening received 19 and writing 20. This compared with the world's average of 19.5 and 20.5, respectively. Koreans did, not surprisingly, beat the world average at reading, 20, compared with a 19.4 global average. On the top of the English language hill were Denmark and the Netherlands, with average scores of 102. Next were Austria and Singapore with 100, followed by Belgium and Germany with 98 and 97. Interestingly, The Philippines, which has adopted English as an official language, like Singapore, ranked 32nd, with an average of 88 points.

Not to pick on Korea too much, let's have a look at how other Asian nations fared. China placed 99th with 76 points, Taiwan at 106th with 73, and Japan 136th with 66; thus placing many Asian countries at the bottom of the hill. These scores are more than just a collection of numbers; they tend to illustrate that, despite a colossal amount of assets devoted to English language instruction, Asians are having a devil of a time learning English as compared to

European and Scandinavian countries. This isn't a fluke nor is it trivial. I will discuss this a bit later.

Speaking of colossal amounts of money devoted to English. Have a go at this: The Bank of Korea has suggested that private English language instruction amounts to four to five trillion KRW (roughly 3,570,792,247 USD), much of which is devoted to taking the TOEIC and TOEFL tests. I've had students take the TOEIC six or seven times. Now, then, the TOEIC test is not free. Do the students pay? No, it's the parents that must bear the financial burden. If you are not undergoing a spit-take after reading these figures, you should be, or at least a jaw-drop. According to TOEIC, Korea is number one in the world for test takers.

What is the upside to all of this, if any? To begin, at the end of World War II the literacy rate in Korea was around 22 percent. These days, the literacy rate is an incredible 98 percent. The downside? Glad you asked. We've discussed the colossal amounts of money Korean's spend on education, but, and perhaps more sobering, is the fact that the system is responsible for a declining birth rate, which is now among the world's lowest. Parents simply cannot continue to fund an increasingly expensive education system for their children, so they are happy to have only one or two children; yet another hurdle to overcome going forward.

If you haven't gotten the idea of just how important English is to Korean society by now, you never will. However, I'll reinforce the fact. English is a never-ending source of power in Korean society. To get into the best schools and corporations requires a near-fluent command of English, and not just speaking, but the other skills as well. It doesn't stop there, however, even after landing that envied corporate position, Koreans must continue to study English to maintain their skills and perhaps climb the ladder to a higher position within the company.

Those of us who have learned and taught a foreign/second language know well just how demanding it is. I know from my teaching experience that many become frustrated and simply give up, or become satisfied with their level. Unfortunately, Koreans that can use English pragmatically are few and far between.

We also know that one of the best ways to learn a language is through immersion, if it is done correctly. Just so, most Koreans lack the time or money to live in an English speaking country. Thus English becomes a dark cloud they must live under for quite some time. On the one hand, it's a source of power, on the other, a source of continuous stress well into adulthood.

The Korean government has taken past actions to increase English instruction in the public schools, increasing contact time to two to three hours per week, depending on the grade level. However, as mentioned previously, 2 or 3 hours per week is absurd.

Past surveys have shown that students and parents are dissatisfied with government actions of increasing English instruction. Related to that, I've lost count of the students I've known, teens and adults, that communicate at a low to mid-intermediate level in English even after more than ten years of study in the public schools. These communicative difficulties continue at universities. And that, readers, is yet another thread: university language instruction is pathetic, and it's that way primarily because of the lack of creativity of the teachers – native and non-native, in the

English language departments as well as their methodologies.

There is a university that has tried to model itself after MIT in the USA: KAIST (Korea Advanced Institute of Science and Technology). In a rather futile, but admirable, attempt to increase their international rank and attract more international students, they experimented with conducting many classes in English. Naturally, no Korean instructor was happy about this, not to mention the students. It has been said that this experiment contributed to four suicides among KAIST students and no end of complaints from the Korean instructors, which is truly one of many downsides of globalization.

I firmly believe that by now you've seen just how important English is to many Koreans. Thousands of hours and just as much money are invested in study every year.

So, how does Korea compare to other non-English speaking nations? In the English Proficiency Index (EPI), conducted by English First (EF), nations are ranked according to their English proficiency level. Results include cultural, social, financial, and historical backgrounds. One interesting result was that Korea ranked 13th among 44 countries in the index. The top Asian country was Malaysia with a 9th place score. Second highest was Hong Kong, while Japan ranked 14th. Not surprisingly, the number one country was Norway. The Scandinavian countries, in general, trade places for number one year after year on the index.

I suppose there is much to be learned from the index. One fact Koreans can take away from the index is that a 13th place rank is pretty dammed good, all things considered. Why are the Scandinavian countries so successful? Perhaps it is because English is one of the most important subjects in school, unlike English in Korea.

As a father of two sons, I find myself continually reminding my sons of the importance of having good English language skills. Even if it means that their Korean language skills suffer. And this has largely come to pass; they do wonderful on their English exams, as absurd as those exams are, but do poorly on Korean exams. I attribute this to the fact that Korean language exams are grammar based, believe it or not.

I also know through research that the Scandinavians set goals regarding English language learning. This goal setting is just as foreign to Korean policymakers as is English. Therein lies one of the reasons for success in Scandinavia. Korea must come to terms with how and why they are putting so much time, effort, and finances into English instruction only to result in a negative ROI.

Before you consider teaching in Korea, I think that it is important to understand why learning English is so challenging to learners. Such discussion can only serve to make you a more aware and knowledgeable teacher. I can't discuss all of the reasons, there are just too many, so I'll discuss the reasons that I believe most salient.

Social stratification and democratic language. Egalitarianism and Stratification

I don't recall where I read it, but it has remained with me for many years: due to its language, Korea can never be a democratic society. This is most certainly debatable. And for the sake of debate, let's compare and contrast English and Korean.

English is most certainly egalitarian. Yes, English language countries do have social stratification, implicit or explicit. The USA, for example, certainly has social status, but little mention of it is made in the English lexicon. English, for all means and purposes, is a language of social equality. English does not stratify, for example, the CEO of Microsoft, or Microsoft's janitorial staff. The language itself is fairly egalitarian across all social classes.

Now then, one of the basic tenants of democracy, as I understand it, is that *"All men are created equal."* Yes, I know, sexist. The English language, despite its man/men prefix and suffix, qualifies this tenant quite well. The language system does not vary according to who you are, your position, or how old you are.

Korean, on the other hand, is the antithesis of English. Korea is an incredibly stratified culture, and the language illustrates that quite well through the use of honorifics. I place a bit of blame on Confucius, the Chinese philosopher of old, but that, too, can be argued. Confucianism in Korea has been much modified over the centuries, so Koreans, it would seem, have created their own philosophy in the guise of Confucianism. Furthermore, Confucianism really has little to do with the educational fervor in modern Korea. That fervor is due more to parents' *survivalist* instincts. Any way you look at it, you'll find that Korea has become a very stratified, inegalitarian society. To illustrate this, the Korean language currently uses different forms (at last count, five) for the social classes. These forms are dropped only by mutual agreement between persons.

As a speaker of an egalitarian language, the use of honorifics when speaking Korean has been incredibly challenging for me. I disdain them, but I sometimes use them nevertheless, despite my distaste for them.

This social stratification harkens way back in history. Korean feudal structure was much worse at that time then it is now. Obviously, Korea no longer has feudal structure; however, it does exist. It exists in the work place; blue collar vs. white collar, old vs. young, those who have been educated at a top university and those who have not; those with BMWs, Mercedes, and those with Kias, Hyundais, and on and on.

This stratification is everywhere; in its social mores, interactions, language and a host of other subtle and obvious ways. Korea has been said to be a *vertical* class society because of its high and low stratification. English speaking countries have been said to be *horizontal* societies because the language does not stratify.

The takeaway from this is that Koreans sometimes find it difficult to use English due to this vertical thinking, which, as many of my students admit, is incredibly challenging to omit. However, once they get the hang of it, many are so relieved that discover that they prefer English because it does not stratify.

Furthermore, the grammar of the languages is in opposition. English has become a very possessive language that places emphasis on the individual and his/her freedom. In Korea, my, mine, are not explicitly expressed. Those *Id* concepts are replaced by *our* – our university, our teacher, our country.

Culture of Ambiguity

When one compares English and Korean, one finds that English is largely unambiguous. English language speakers are direct to a point, which sometimes offends Koreans who comprehend English but are not culturally informed. How can you tell? When Koreans are embarrassed or nervous, they chuckle. This can be very confusing to newbies in Korea. Many newbies might think *"What did I say that was funny?"* when, in fact, *nothing* was funny.

This is context driven, so to avoid confrontations, be aware of the context of the conversation. If you do, you'll come to understand this conundrum.

Moreover, English language grammar, due to its directness, really doesn't require long strings to get the message across. A simple sentence is often enough; one subject, one verb. Yet, when I listen to Korean speakers in real time or watch the Korean subtitles to an English language film, I'm often taken aback by how long the translations are. A simple sentence in English becomes a complex one in Korean, due to its indirectness.

And, so, Koreans have yet another challenge/conflict to overcome when learning English; two very diverse languages at odds with one another nearly everywhere: in business negotiations, government policies and politics, in the classroom, and between family members. English and Korean are uncomfortable bedfellows as illustrated in, for example, business, wherein there really is no room for error. This explains why there are so many teaching opportunities for business English teachers. The challenge is to overcome the Korean desire for ambiguity in language and learn how to say what you mean and mean what you say.

Finally, by way of an example of indirect speech, I'm amazed when a Korean speaker says to me in Korean: "It seems (or appears) to be cold today" when in fact it's absolutely freezing.

Emotive Society

That Koreans are an emotional people would be a colossal understatement. Koreans are bipolar poster children, or so it would seem.

Recently, I witnessed two cars approaching each other on a one-way farm road. One car flashed its lights at the other, which means that it had the right-of-way, but the other car continued until they finally met each other, bumper to bumper. After a few minutes wait, the drivers got out of their cars and began arguing about right-of-way. As is the Korean way, shouting eventually gave way to physical confrontation, although not serious. After about 10 minutes of this, both returned to their cars. I thought, finally, they've worked it out. However, the cars did not move, and neither did I. I wanted to see how this would play out. After sitting in my truck for 20 minutes waiting for someone to move, I simply gave up. God knows how long those two idiots sat there.

Would this have happened in the West? I imagine that had it happened, the drivers would have worked it out in a calm, rational manner. Conversely, knowing how violence driven Westerners can be...well, you be the judge.

Suffice to say, it could be posited that English speakers are direct, even when emotional. When emotion is present, it is largely used only when all else fails or for dramatic purposes.

In contrast, Koreans are the whiners of the world. And I don't use the term lightly, or in any culturally insensitive way. There exist certain intonation patterns that drive me to drink...well, more than I normally do. One pattern is found at the end of a request, plea, or from frustration. It seems like childish plea for attention. This is usually followed by tears, screaming, or physical confrontation, just as in my example above. I just can't imagine a Korean speaker arguing a point in Korean without that damned whining intonation; yet another cultural conflict. More than a few of my Korean friends have been in fights, again not serious, and, as the confrontation becomes more serious, I hear that intonation pattern in nearly every statement they make. I also hear that same pleading intonation pattern with my learners, despite many years of learning English.

Put simply, it's difficult, if not impossible to plea using a language such as English, although my sons, when they were very young, did a pretty good job of it. As adults, however, we simply don't have the vocabulary or the intonation for it. And, so, Koreans find it difficult to learn that they cannot use English for emotionalism, so they often either give up or move on to physical confrontation. What is also interesting, from a pragmatic point of view, is that if the listener tries to remain calm in the face of this whining emotionalism, the one whining gets even more upset, to the point of becoming violent. I have had much experience with this, sadly.

Despite these language/cultural differences, I do see hope. I sometimes teach English to dormitory students at one of the local universities. These young people seem to have overcome many of the above conflicts. In fact, I sometimes feel that I'm back home conversing with native speakers.

Welcome to Zombie Hell.

2. States Parties shall respect and promote the right of the child to participate fully in cultural and artistic life and shall encourage the provision of appropriate and equal opportunities for cultural, artistic, recreational and leisure activity.

– Article 31, Clause 2 – Declaration of the Rights of the Child – United Nations

When I think of Hagwons and Korean children, a comic drawn by an anonymous Korean student comes to mind. I mistakenly found this comic on the internet while doing some related research. In this comic, a Korean secondary school student is having a blast playing baseball with his friends; in short, doing what children do best. Suddenly, his friends tell him they must quit play and return home at once. It is time for the hagwon.

Although confused, the boy shrugs it off and returns home to parents awaiting his return, arms akimbo. They are quick to tell him that all of the other children in their friend's families attend four or five hagwons while he attends none. This is simply unacceptable, particularly to the Tiger Mother. And, so, for that reason and that reason alone, he is sent to study at a hagwon. This harkens back to my discussion on the characteristics of the Tiger Mother.

His first day at the hagwon is pure, unmitigated hell. He is but one among a host of children with zombie postures and appearance. Much as I would like to continue, I'll refer you to the comic here:

226

http://www.flickr.com/photos/bpbp0709/sets/721576041
14868975/

What, then, is my point? Welcome to every child's hell: the hagwon. I know I've discussed it at length, but more needs to be said.

The hagwon culture in Korea is simply inexcusable. Children are not only forced to endure more study after school, but study material far beyond their maturity level. Child psychology and emotional well-being are simply too much for Koreans to understand. I would be remiss to say that, even if they did, the status quo would continue. Benevolent Ministry of Education officials come and go, but meanwhile nothing changes. Korean parents, particularly the Tiger Mother, have in common short-sightedness in that they continue the nasty habit of keeping of with the Lees. Many simply cannot think for themselves, god forbid.

Teachers teaching core subjects in these hagwons, not including English, are really pretty much 'bot types. They lecture, lecture, lecture, and lecture some more. If a child simply cannot understand, that child will be left behind. If a child doesn't do homework, the teacher dishes out corporal punishment.

The children learn; they learn to hate the hagwon and the teachers in it, including English teachers if they don't keep it together. You're going to find that unless you are a dynamic, flexible teacher, children will come to hate your classes. Korean children, understandably, are simply not interested in learning English despite all the nonsense of officials, mothers and fathers. Those endorsements are mythology to children.

And it's incredibly easy to understand why. They see no reason for it. They do it because they are forced to do it. For Korean children, hagwons are simply another in a series of after-school extracurricular activities. This does not make for emotionally stable children.

Korean Tiger Mothers believe that if they tell their children that learning English is good for their future, their career, their country, and that it is the lingua franca of the world, that their children will magically transform into English language learning monsters. I've even heard Tiger Mothers explain to their children that English competence will mean happiness or lack thereof. Even if this were somehow true, the fact remains that children simply don't give a rat's ass about their mother's lectures regarding English. If you, dear readers, had any childhood at all, you'll understand why.

Furthermore, Korean children are usually too exhausted from what seems an endless cycle of hagwons, lessons, lectures, anger, disappointment, failure, and loss of face. After-school English classes are simply another rotten apple they are force-fed. And failure is *not* an option. Tiger Mothers relentlessly push their children not to fail, not realizing that failure is part of the human experience, and, if proper perspective and a parent with even half a useable brain is present, failure can also lead to discovery, maturity, and better future outcomes. Ask a Korean middle or high school student if he/she has ever contemplated suicide because of failure and you'll quickly discover that many of them have. *"Thanks, mom! I'm going to the roof of the apartment for a little private time. Swoosh!"* If it sounds like I'm making a value judgment, then you would be correct.

What's more, every culture has requirements whether food, fun, money, or jobs, just as they do distractions: games, drinking, sports. Needs and distractions, folks. But for Korean children, being force-fed English is neither.

You'll hear it from the kids, from their teachers, from everyone but the Tiger Mothers. *"Why must we learn English?"* is the never-ending question among Korean children. I imagine, hell, I know in the past, when Korea was not so saturated with all things English, learning English from an NSET was undoubtedly the most exciting event to happen in quite some time. Indeed, recall my words on celebrity status of the NSET when I first came to Korea. These days, however, with the over-saturation of all things Western, Korean kids simply don't give a damn about who is teaching them. English has become the enemy, an enemy that will simply not go away, that will keep coming at them, even into adulthood.

Children, as I know them, and I know them well, lack the ability to see beyond their next adventure, usually some kind of game or an event with a friend. However, the next (mis)adventure in Korea usually means the hagwon. Whether it is English, math, or science, their next adventure is derailed and in place of that are stress, fear of failure, and their Tiger Mothers. English competence may have rewards some fine day, but *someday* is of no interest to children. What is important to children is the *here and now.* I also know from experience that public school teachers have no mercy on those who get behind or slack off a bit. Recall that teachers use corporal punishment, verbal threats, rage, and a host of other weapons at their disposal. With that in mind, it's easy to understand how discipline rules the day. It's little wonder, then, that the after-school hagwons lack the element of law and order that the public schools don't. Many after-school teachers complain about misbehavior, uncooperative behavior, and unmotivated students. Tell a Korean teacher he/she is a poor teacher in the public school system (like one of my sons correctly did) and that teacher will raise no end of hell. And that's a major complaint of mine; vertical thinking cultures tolerate no challenges to character, position, or otherwise, despite the fact that those challenges and opinions are dead on. This is not a Confucian ideal; this is Confucianism gone awry. Take Panmal – informal speaking style – for example. Use panmal on an older Korean male, for example, and he'll have a meltdown. After 17 years in this country, I still rarely use formal style. If I have to use formal style, I will simply speak English. You don't earn my respect because you are older or have a government job; you earn my respect by respecting me and acting like a decent human being, culture or no culture.

But I digress. Hell, my own sons hated winter and summer vacations because their mother was too damned busy lining up their next study program, which was largely a waste of time and money. Let's micromanage our children to hell and to hell with a childhood seems to be the credo for the day, week, month, year, lifetime?

And I would be remiss if I neglected to add that happiness of Korean students between the ages of ten and 18, as measured by two Korean institutes - the Bang Jeong-hwan Foundation and the Institute for Social Development studies at Yonsei University - was the lowest on the index among the 23 OECD member states for the third year in a row.

One of the negative outcomes of this is that children are raised to be dependent and lazy. The Korean adults who have graduated university that I hang with are certainly guilty of this. They absolutely abhor physical labor and cannot understand why I am building a house with my own hands instead of hiring someone to do it. This attitude makes me sick to the point that I have infinitely more respect for the day-laborer/farmer than I do for the professor.

And so it is that English study is the stuff of nightmares. Nightmares for all involved: teachers, children, parents, and government officials. Is it little wonder, then, that test results are so poor?

What should you take away from this? Simply that children learn best when they are allowed to be children, so remember to use a variety of fun and games in the form of songs, rhythm, storytelling, play-acting, and so forth (Think Finland). If children are forced to learn English, at least let them have some quality time before they are off to the next hagwon.

Also, and I can't stress this enough, English study in Korea has become more of a trend than anything else. What I've seen, and continue to see today, is that those who do have English competence rarely use it. They have forgotten the maxim of learning: if you don't use it, you lose it. Thus, all the time, money, energy, blood, sweat, and tears have been nothing more than an exercise in futility.

Yet another negative outcome of this lack of childhood results in sub-average university students. University students, free of their Tiger Mothers, get seriously busy; busy catching up with their lost childhood. Heavy drinking and gaming become the norm, while study is seriously neglected; ergo, sub-average.

And, so, there exists a cycle of ineptness beginning with parents who are dissatisfied with public school education believing, with some credibility, that public education is not in their children's best academic interest. This dissatisfaction is what gave fuel to the hagwon fire. This is particularly salient at the high school level, where students begin gearing up for the CSAT – the college entrance exam.

This gearing up comes as yet another dark cloud that the Korean parental unit must live under. Any Korean Tiger Mother worth her stripes will willingly fund her children's hagwon/private tutoring fees, to the tune of USD $600 to $1,200 monthly.

Yet another failing of Korean mothers is their willingness to accept low standards in hagwons. Do they ever check if the director can actually *speak* English? Once in a blue moon, readers. These mothers rely on flashy brochures, word of mouth, trends and promises of easy-to-learn English language programs. Who bothers to educate these mothers? Who Okayed this?

While I'm on the soap box, here's another gem, one in which I have personal experience. In 2003, the United Nations committee on the Rights of the Child (yes, it does exist) stated that the irrational educational system in Korea violated children's' "*rights to play.*" I continually ask myself, "*What rights?*" for they are nonexistent in Korea. How extremely rare, and yet wonderful, it is to see a Korean middle or high school student fishing, hiking, biking, or simply wandering for the sake of wandering. Free time is seen as laziness. "*Hey, son, how dare you have fun! What's wrong with you? Aren't you ready for another 14 hour day? You're so lazy!"*

And, yes, this teacher also condemns Korea of systemic child abuse. Childhood and old age are really the only times in one's life that certain freedoms are taken for granted. Childhood should be a time of growth through study and recreation. Let's get real, it is our youth that many of us most fondly remember when we become old. Those memories are sometimes the only pleasant memories we have of life. To be robbed of them would be similar to having Alzheimer's disease. Not a pleasant comparison, but the truth is not always pleasant.

Just as Korean university students become sub-average because of their hyper-Tiger Mothers, so do many middle and high school children. Any and all free time is used on the smart phone, to the point of more than one student walking directly into traffic while texting. Text this: do not pass go, do not collect $100, your mother has sent you to the grave. Indeed, smart phones have become indispensable to Korean students. Is this due to having no childhood recreation? It's certainly worthy of discussion.

All things hagwon were not so do or die back in the dictator days of, say, former president Chun Doo-hwan, (1979 to 1988) whose daughter, sadly, is currently president of Korea. Chun banned all private institutes with the goal in mind that each student was responsible for his/her own learning, and that students have equal access to higher education. Despite that attempt, private tutors simply adapted; they moved underground and charged exorbitant fees. Tutors, students, and parents endured risks believing that they would never be caught by the Chun administration.

Not a bad idea, right? Yet, in the 1990s, the ban was lifted and Voila! A billion dollar industry sprang back to life in all its guts and glory. High test scores were the promise of the period then, just as they are now.

Worst of all, as mentioned previously, the fertility rate in Korea has steadily fallen since 1960, when the average was six children per family to 1.15 in 2009. One wonders, then, if Korean officials and citizens are aware of the enormity of this of this demographic catastrophe. Seen in this light, the educational culture of Korea is an infectious disease. This is not how a country competes in an increasingly globalized world.

My Take on Korea and its People

Given that I've lived in Korea for 17 years, readers will probably have a few questions regarding my take on the culture and its people, as well they might. Similar to any culture in which I've lived, I've found this one to have positive and negative aspects, obviously. The big takeaway? The people here, although they will most certainly argue this, are nothing special. One of my Korean friends claims that Korean people have *"warm hearts."* My experience living in various cultures has shown me that Korean hearts are no warmer than others. What you will find, however, is that many Korean people can be sullen to the point of scowling, which can be quite disconcerting if you're from a small town where everyone knows each other, which also has its drawbacks. The younger generation, however, born of a different generation and a different outlook than the sullen folks, have an entirely different demeanor. They did not have to endure the brutal hardships of the Japanese occupation or the Korean War. To be honest, this sullenness is not directed toward foreigners, only.

If Korean people do have warm hearts, foreigners are excluded from it unless you become a good friend with a Korean. Even then, there is nothing remarkable about that friendship. When I think of friendship, my thoughts travel back to my time in Mexico, where a friend – at least during the years I lived there- is a friend for life; where the credo is *"A friend in need is a friend indeed."* Where even the poorest family will invite you stay and share a meal, however meager it may be. Alas, I know it's unfair to compare cultures, but we all do it, either implicitly or explicitly.

When I'm away from Korea, it is certainly not the people I miss; it's the little things that can be found only in Korea: the food, traditional music (Pansori aside); traditional architecture, the absolute vibrancy of the communities. Taking a walk through of any of the small communities in the state where I'm from is like taking a walk in a graveyard - lifelessness abounds. The last time I visited my folks, I was astounded at the difference in vibrancy between the two counties; at least where I'm from. And consider that Korea has no gun violence (not restricted to Korea, I know). Finally, my house of stone and logs!

What do I *not* miss? The driving would be first on my list. I would probably have an entirely different outlook on Korean people if I simply gave up driving, however impractical that may be. I can't believe how a reasonably intelligent people can morph into total idiots when behind the wheel. Recall my thoughts on individualism and how toxic it can be? Well, driving behavior is the best example I can find in this culture. I once read, and I can't recall the reference, that one of the credos Koreans seem to live by: *"If I don't know you, I don't see you."* Hmm, certainly seems to explain driving behavior. Americans, it can be said, kill each other with guns; Koreans kill each other with cars. Yes, I know well that poor driving habits are not restricted to Korea. Much of Asia is driver-challenged.

Next on list would be greed. I've had some really negative experiences with this one. Where other cultures in which I've lived would probably forgive and forget minor incidents, Koreans rarely do. I attribute this to the culture's survivalist instincts. People here would never miss the opportunity to make a quick buck. To wit: I once took my focus off driving in heavy traffic and met the rear bumper of the car in front of me. By met, I mean touched lightly. The driver of the other car jumped out of his car and began examining his rear bumper, which was unscathed. However, he was able to find a blemish, which was obviously there prior to the incident and so took advantage of it. Long story short, I ended up dishing out $50.00 for a blemish that wasn't from my car. Bear in mind that this is *not* an isolated incident, there are others that were much worse, but it pains me greatly to recall them in print. Indeed, these incidents have given me a rather skewed outlook on the people here.

Koreans have taken the term *"survivalist"* to new heights. Just as Western people are brought up to purse an elusive kind of security, primarily through the acquisition of material goods and the money to buy them, Koreans also see financial well-being as happiness and success. The primary means to this end is via education, which has created a Darwinian nightmare, as far as this author is concerned. Students begin competing as early as middle school. Those that do well in middle and high school may have a chance at economic *survival*, which doesn't necessarily equate with success and happiness, as you have already seen.

I would be remiss if I didn't mention how loud Koreans can be. Korean people believe Western people are loud, but I wonder if Korean people ever listen to themselves and those around them. Why in hell I have to listen to someone's phone conversation 40 meters away is a never-ending mystery. Koreans, particularly men, don't speak, they yell into the phone. I once asked a Korean friend why this behavior exists, and he honestly didn't know, nor was he aware of it until I pointed it out.

And this issue of noise certainly applies in the countryside, also. It's not just the people, but the truck vendors, the community PA system, the Soju drunks, the traffic, the nearby factories, the fighter jets, the farm machinery...the list goes on. "Land of Morning Calm?" More like "Land of Morning Chaos." Unless you are truly isolated – think islands – you'll not have much morning calm. But then, to be fair, I was raised in the boonies where it was *too* quiet.

And then I'm reminded of the garbage one can find almost *everywhere*. Although I'm not Korean, I still get pissed when I see people throw their garbage in the streets, countryside, and particularly on the ocean beaches. You really can't get away from someone's garbage in Korea. What's really interesting is that Korea has a wonderful system of recycling waste, so you can't help but wonder. I understand that there are no waste receptacles in the countryside and beaches, where many Koreans go to vacation, but why not simply bring garbage back and recycle it? It's entirely doable. I live near a university that I once taught at, so I sometimes visit professors on campus that I came to know during my tenure there. When driving through the small community in front of the university, I'm always taken aback – even after 17 years - by the amount of garbage to be found everywhere. It's as if the community is swimming in refuse. What are people thinking? They aren't, and that's the problem.

One of the things this nutty Westerner does is to refuse the use of pesticides and herbicides on his land and fruit trees. The villagers just don't get it. This is a country that has a love affair with toxic chemicals, and anyone who doesn't use them just doesn't fit in with preconceived notions of how to deal with pests. And why all the blank looks when I ask the villagers what their ancestors used to use prior to the introduction of chemicals? It harkens back to greed and a decided lack of creativity and study, not to mention downright laziness.

To offer some balance to what seems a biased take on Korea, you should know that I'm one of the worst critics of the USA. Indeed, I could write a 600 page book on gun violence alone. This is particularly salient because I'm writing this a week after the shooting at Sandy Hook Elementary School in Connecticut. In light of that, my criticism of Korea is light-hearted.

Conclusion

The conclusion, which I debated for many months, is in two parts. The first part includes a look at Western economies as they are and will be in the years to come, and the second a look at Korea's economic status. I've include the first part because, at least in Korea, citizens suffer very little of the many economic woes that Western economies do. This is perhaps the number two reason why I have continued to stay in Korea rather than return to the West. After reading what I and others have to say about the state of economic affairs, particularly in the USA, you may want to reconsider your lack of a college degree, or your unreasonable emotional attachment to the West, and see the West for what it is and what it will continue to be well into the future.

Pretty much all USA citizens are aware of the financial crisis of 2008. How could we not? Since then, more folks have been forced to accept government handouts during the last four years than ever before. Not only that, but the Federal Reserve continues to create money out of thin air to stimulate the economy. Only lately has the fed been trying to stem the flow of money printing.

Because the economy is not improving, despite what the bureaucrats say, more people have stayed unemployed for a much longer period of time, thus more dependent on government. By way of example, consider that the use of food stamps has increased 46 percent since the beginning of 2009 to July of 2012. As people have stayed unemployed for a longer period of time, they have become more dependent on government. In January of 2009, 32.0

million people were on some form of food stamps. The number now sits at around 46.7 million.

Those of you who argue that the unemployment rate has improved need to open your eyes to reality. Many large-cap companies are already announcing cuts to their workforce, and it's not just U.S companies showing concern; the multinationals are struggling as well. If you need evidence of this, look no further: E. I. du Pont de Nemours and Company, 1,500 employees; United Technologies Corporation: overall budget cuts of 20%; HSBC Holdings plc: 30,000 jobs. The Goldman Sachs Group, Inc. will reduce the number of partners in the company; so much for trillions of dollars given to world economies since 2009. Two steps forward, three steps back.

You also need to keep in mind that there are more than 12.0 million people unemployed for less than 27 weeks, and another 5.0 million who have been working part-time because they can't find full-time employment. Naturally, the government would like you believe that the "*official*" unemployment rate has fallen, but the real unemployment rate, when factoring in those who have given up looking for work and those who work part-time jobs but want full-time jobs, is a recipe for disaster.

I recently read a survey done by Employee Benefit Research Institute. In that survey, Americans are clearly becoming concerned about their ability to retire in comfort. The number one and two concerns, unsurprisingly, are job uncertainty and debt. Forty-two percent of the respondents believe that job uncertainty is the biggest hurdle to financial success. Likewise, 60 percent of the workers reported that they have total household savings and investments of less than $25,000. Which begs the question: how can there be consumer spending growth under these circumstances? Consumer spending, so necessary to a healthy economy, only increases when consumers are happy with the economy: jobs, savings, investments.

As of this writing, consumers are *not* happy with any of the above. For folks to spend, you need a healthy dose of consumer confidence, which has continued on a downward spiral even after multiple rounds of quantitative easing and the government throwing good money after bad to stimulate the economy.

I've also read that roughly 100 California dairy farmers are shutting down because they are facing financial hardships due to weak demand for milk and lower profit margins. Are folks actually decreasing spending on dairy products? Hard to fathom, but certainly possible.

The point I'm trying to make is that the U.S. economy is still in a hell of a mess, and millions of folks are still suffering as a result.

THE USA IS NOT ALONE

Central banks worldwide are struggling to cope with a slowdown in the global economy. Said slowdown is spreading like a virus. Destruction of wealth is becoming a global issue beginning with the financial crisis in the USA and moving to the Eurozone credit crisis, which made the situation even worse.

To counter the global slowdown, banks, not only in developed countries but emerging economies also, have kept interest rates artificially near zero for years, all to no avail. Thus, one option remains, particularly those wanting to lower their currency to encourage their exports: print more money.

The central banks in the global economy want lending to increase. Their reasoning is that if lending increases, demand will increase. What they are missing is that big businesses are worried about the many uncertainties today and in the future. These corporations are nesting on a record amount of cash as a result of not making investments or hiring, so they obviously do not need to borrow. This has created a *"have money, afraid to invest, will not borrow,"* mentality among companies. This mentality could continue well into the future.

And consider scenarios such as this: a federal program that began as a last resort for a few million hungry people has grown into an economic lifeline for entire towns. Spending on SNAP (food stamps) has doubled in the past four years and tripled in the past decade, surpassing $78 billion last year. A record 47 million Americans receive the benefit—including 13,752 in Woonsocket, one third of the town's population. The Keynesian policies of tax, spend, borrow, print, subsidize, and regulate are what got the USA into this mess in the first place, and the boneheads in Washington think more of the same will magically save you.

Point is, none of that has washed up on the shores of South Korea. Yes, there most certainly an economic slowdown, but it has had little noticeable effect on the demand for English language teachers. Hundreds of teachers are still hired every year, and the wage, although not noticeably increased in the last eight years, is reliable. Everywhere I look in Korea, I see infrastructure improvements, hundreds of newly constructed high-rise apartments, new highways and repair of old ones, new businesses opening every day, crowded shopping centers, a reasonable social welfare system, low taxation, and *so* much more. Need more evidence? Hell, if you're so moved by Western culture that you can't contemplate leaving it, you need to see a shrink. There just isn't any logical reason for living in poverty when you have so many financially expedient choices!

Thus, I hope I've offered you compelling reasons why you may want to consider teaching English; and if not in Korea, than elsewhere. Readers, things simply aren't going to get better in the West. The USA, for example, will *never* be what it once was prior to the financial crisis of 2008. So, get that school loan, finish your degree or begin one and teach English.

I've tried to cover everything you should know before you make that decision, but I've left out a lot of cultural issues aside from teaching because there are hundreds of websites that you can refer to that will answer all of your questions on not only culture, but what to bring, survival Korean language, bus and subway, clothing, and much more. You can also email, Skype, or ask on the Seonsang.com website forum, and I'll be more than happy to point you in the right direction.

As to teaching in Korea, there is little to take away other than to experience a different culture. As stated earlier, the people here are no better, nor no worse than any other nation that I've lived and taught. However, I know from experience that there are countries where teaching English is a much more positive undertaking than Korea; usually undeveloped countries where learning is seen as a gift that not all can, or will, obtain. As you have seen, English in Korea has become such a negative experience for most everyone involved. It wasn't always like that. Korea, prior to becoming developed, was also one of those countries where learning a foreign language, particularly the lingua franca of the world, was not seen as such a burden. These days, English in Korea seems to have become lingua nongrata, due to the many reasons that I've discussed.

Most of all, I am very aware that I've not painted a very pretty picture of teaching English in Korea. I have a bone to pick, of that I'm aware. At the risk of too much information, the culture of the Tiger Mother was one of the primary factors leading this author's dysfunctional marriage. Old cultures like Korea are so damned culturally bound that thinking outside cultural norms is an enormous undertaking. Factor in personal baggage, and you've got a relationship that spells doom. Korean women, in general, wear the pants in the family, so to speak. This is particularly true of the Tiger Mother/wife. Any challenges to the would-be matriarch are not tolerated. In Korea, the male role is simply that of a wage slave. Is it any wonder that Korean males are often the majority culture in sex tours to the Philippines and Thailand? Having a Korean wife will do that. Most Korean women live for four things: eating, sleeping, watching TV, and shopping; but more about that in my next book.

The fact is, if you are looking for a rewarding experience as an NSET, you may want to forgo teaching here in favor of one of the many countries that still look forward to learning English. You may not make as good of a wage, (I was sometimes paid in chickens) but the enthusiasm of the children you teach will more than make up for the loss. It can, and perhaps *will be* the most memorable experience of your life.

I imagine it could still be like that in Korea if not for Tiger Mothers, the CSAT, and the importance Koreans place on high TOEIC/OPIK scores, to name just a few.

Of major importance is the fact that it's very easy to save money in Korea; depending, naturally, on how attached you are to the night life. If you decide to stay here for four or five years, you will have a pretty respectable bank account. Related to that, I can't think of many countries where a recent graduate can teach for 30 hours a week and make a pretty damn good wage without having to spend a lifetime in college studying teacher training to become licensed. Really, folks, it's amazing when you stop to think about it. So, while I may dump on Korea, it offers a lifestyle that many only dream of.

When I sometimes think about returning to the USA, I become very ambivalent; I just can't imagine myself living that safe, relatively boring life while my life ebbs by. I've also come to like being different in a very homogenous culture. I used to get incredibly bothered when Koreans drilled holes in me with those sullen eyes, but these days I rather enjoy it. Returning to the USA would mean becoming anonymous, which is not my idea of a good time.

More to the point, what would I do? I'm middle aged, so there would be little or nothing for me by way of employment. I would, like thousands of other middle aged folks, have to find work outside of what I love. How about becoming a greeter at Wal-Mart? No, thank you.

And above all remember this: all the institutions that made America tolerable – including a belief in capitalism, individualism, self-reliance and the restraints of the Constitution – are now only historical artifacts. Post-9/11 has turned the US into a national security state, I'm ashamed to say. And watch what happens post-Boston Marathon bombing.

If you do decide to come to Korea, please keep in touch! I'm here for you, and I will help you in any way possible. I look forward to visiting with you in Jeonbuk!

Talk to you soon,

Dwight H. Gauer

Index

About the Author

Itinerant teacher, craftsman, beer aficionado, and father of two incredibly handsome sons, Tristan and Remy, Dwight H. Gauer has been fully immersed in Korean culture for the past 17 years. He currently lives in a rural village of 78 people in Jeonbuk Province where he is building a house, rustic furniture, and tentative relations with the villagers, despite the fact that they continue to walk into his house unannounced.

For the best Korean Job Board Websites, including Mr. Park's jobs-korea.org, please email Dwight. He would be more than happy to help you on your way. Also, Dwight is planning a language institute review service for people looking for "safe" teaching jobs in Korea, Stay tuned for that on Dwight's website:

http://www.teach-korea-english.com

Prior to teaching in Korea, Dwight taught in Mexico, Belize, and Guatemala. He dreams of returning to Mexico one day to continue life in Topolobanpo where beer, mescal, tequila, and senoritas thrive.

Stay tuned for Dwight's upcoming novel on life in a Korean village: The Halmoni Wars

To talk to Dwight, simply email him at:

iksanshi@yahoo.com

CPSIA information can be obtained
at www.ICGtesting.com
Printed in the USA
BVHW041136100221
599803BV00009B/80